Under an
AFRICAN
Sky

THE UNUSUAL LIFE OF A MISSIONARIES' KID
IN ETHIOPIA

Julene Hodges Schroeder

Under an AFRICAN Sky

THE UNUSUAL LIFE OF A MISSIONARIES' KID IN ETHIOPIA

Julene Hodges Schroeder

Summer Bay Press

Summer Bay Press

Under an African Sky
The Unusual Life of a Missionaries' Kid in Ethiopia

Copyright © 2013 Julene Hodges Schroeder
Interior Design by Wendy Dewar Hughes
Cover Design by Wendy Dewar Hughes
Editing by Carolee Hodges Harbour and Wendy Dewar Hughes

ISBN: 978-1-927626-26-9
Digital ISBN: 978-1-927626-27-6

Summer Bay Press
#14 - 1884 Heath Road
Agassiz, B.C. V0M 1A2

Library and Archives Canada Cataloguing in Publication
Schroeder, Julene, 1951-

Dedication

To my most precious Mom and Daddy.
There are no words to describe how much I love
and am grateful for you.

And to my siblings, who shared this wonderful, unusual life
with me.
I love you with all my heart.

Many Thanks

To Murray, Brian and Carolee. Thank you so much for supplying me with your letters and answering my questions about the years before I was old enough to remember. And Carolee, how can I ever thank you for your untold hours of brilliant editing? You not only have flawless grammar and write exceptionally well but added so many details and corrected things I had remembered wrongly. It was a joint labour of love.

To Marcia – I felt like a multi-millionaire the day you found the Agaro memoirs and our slides of Ethiopia! Thank you so much for all the work you went to in order to locate them for me.

To Wendy Dewar Hughes, my darling cousin, publisher, editor, who designed the interior and cover. You helped me immeasurably from beginning to end. I would never have been able to do this without your coaching on how to use action verbs, take out adverbs and qualifiers and make it far more interesting. Thank you for your astounding expertise in the whole writing and publishing process.

To my dear Bingham classmate, Laura Jacobson Toews, for your lovely artwork on Mom's poem – on the last page – that my siblings and I all have hanging in our homes now, only in gorgeous colour.

To Joy Anderson Harper, Nancy Ackley Ruth and Wendy Leighton Boyle, my beloved "Bingham Belles," whose love always encouraged me to keep going, even when I had acute writer's block. I can never express how happy I am that you are back in my life to stay!

To my sweet friend, Christina Freeman Grafe. Thank you so much for urging me to write, telling me that I had this story in me. You were my inspiration and cheerleader from the very beginning of the whole process.

To my beloved husband, Greg – you have been the perfect, most understanding and gracious husband for this missionaries' kid all these years and I love you so much.

And now to my kids, Mara, Blake and Clarke, Getu and Fiker Alem, thank you for reading this to your own children, so you and they will know about the wonderful, blessed life your mom and her family enjoyed in Ethiopia.

Table of Contents

Chapter One

—∞—

An Unusual Life

I wonder what it would be like to ride in a sleigh?

I gazed out the classroom window, chin in hand, as the teacher's voice droned in the background. Outside, the dry-season-brown grass stretched to the eucalyptus forests that surrounded our boarding school compound in what was yet another sunny Ethiopian day, always the same pleasant temperature. *In one more week I will be going home - to my very favourite place on earth,* I thought.

Pulling my attention back, I admired the Christmas decorations hanging all around the classroom. Scenes of churches with steeples, quaint villages covered in snow and holly and ivy borders covered the bulletin board, in stark contrast to the summery day outside. I especially liked the "little town of Bethlehem" Matthew Hagen had sketched across a long blackboard at the side of the room. I loved the sweet Christmassy feeling it gave me every time I looked at it.

It was the end of November at Bingham Academy and we were writing our exams before we would go on our Christmas holidays. After classes, in our dorms, we packed and re-packed our suitcases, talking non-stop of all the fun things we planned to do when we went home to our mission stations.

"Hosanna has been my home for twelve years – that's most of my life," I said to my dorm mate, Chris, feeling a pang of sadness. This could be my last holiday at our home in Hosanna.

1

"I don't even want to think about the future. I just want to enjoy every minute of this holiday and not have a single thought about Bingham, not one!"

All over Ethiopia, our dads were packing provisions into their Land Rovers and Jeeps to make the long and tortuous treks from their mission stations, preparing to descend on the Addis Ababa mission Headquarters en masse.

When the last day of school finally arrived, they drove out to Bingham Academy and watched our Christmas program. We had practised long and hard for the program all November and now it was time for us to walk down the path, away from the rest of the school buildings, into the fragrant eucalyptus forest where the Gospel Chapel stood like a little church. There our guests sat on the wooden benches with faces beaming as they watched us act out the Christmas story. When the program was over, these dads scooped up their children, piled them and their luggage into their cars and set off for home. Christmas holidays had begun!

Sharilyn and I didn't have to make the dusty two-day trip to Hosanna by car because this time we could go by plane. Daddy drove my little sister and me to Headquarters where we spent the night.

Early the next morning, we took a taxi out to the airport and saw a line-up of Ethiopian Airlines planes on the tarmac with their familiar green, yellow and red stripes and the lion on the tail. I dashed out to our DC3 in the chilly air, shivering as I clutched the front of my sweater close to me, and climbed aboard the plane for our forty-five minute trip to my idea of heaven. Home! I turned around in my seat and pressed my forehead against the small window behind the narrow, metal bench I was strapped onto, and we took off. Miles of beautiful

2

Ethiopian scenery passed beneath us until the long, familiar, grassy airstrip finally came into view.

The plane swooped low over the grass to scatter herd boys and their cattle from the field before it could land. When it looked safe enough, we landed, bumping along the grass and rolling to a stop beside a long windsock. Peering out of the plane window, I could see my mom, almost jumping off the ground as she waved to us. The door finally opened and we tumbled down the steps into her arms, squealing and laughing. We hadn't seen her for more than three months. *How many times over the past term at boarding school have I dreamed of this moment?* I thought. *And now it is really here!*

Daddy gathered our suitcases from the plane, tossed them into the back of the Land Rover, and we all stood to watch and wave at the DC3 as it took off, barely skimming the trees, on the way to its next stop.

Jumping into the car, we set off, lurching along the ruts in the thick, wiry "doofa" grass to our station, a mile away from the airport and Hosanna town. Talking non-stop and interrupting each other, Sharilyn and I wanted to know about everything that we had missed while away at boarding school in Addis Ababa.

"Mom, do we have a Christmas tree?"

"How is Auntie Fiona?"

"Are we going to Ato Bekulla's house to eat injera and wut soon?"

"Is Bilcha excited we're coming?" (We felt sure the dog must know by now that we were about to arrive.)

"Everyone is sure happy about holiday time." Mom said, laughing as she turned around from the front seat. "The kids are thrilled to go home, the parents are thrilled to have them

3

back and the teachers are thrilled to have them go!"

When we drove into our yard, we hopped out of the Land Rover to follow Mom, who always had surprises waiting for us, while Daddy retrieved our luggage. Sure enough, Mom led us to our bedroom, where she had made us matching curtains and bedspreads from bright, flowered material she had found in the market. We squealed with delight and flopped onto our beds, gazing around our beloved bedroom, where we spent so little time during the year.

When we heard barking, we jumped up and raced to the back door. Bilcha had come to meet us, yipping and wagging her tail so wildly we thought she might tip right over. She was only allowed to have her two front paws on the kitchen floor at the back door but her tail was wagging so hard, it was a wonder she was able to keep her back end where it belonged while Sharilyn and I hugged her.

Mattiose, our hard-working cook, with his dark, laughing eyes, grinned at our excitement as he put steaming hot food on the table. *Dinnertime at home!* I could hardly bear the thrill of it.

While we were eating, Daddy put down his fork. "You know that Mr. Ohman is retiring as Mission Director and has asked me to let my name stand when the Council votes for a new Director for East Africa?" he said, looking at each of us.

"Mmm-hm," I answered, my mouth full of spaghetti.

"Well, if that were to happen, we would have to move to Addis in about April…"

Sharilyn interrupted, "Does that mean that we'd get to live at Headquarters with you?"

"Well," answered Mom, "you'd be able to come home from Bingham on weekends."

"Yay!" shouted Sharilyn, raising her fork in the air and

4

bouncing up and down in her chair.

As excited as I was that we might be able to see our parents every weekend, my mind was troubled. I would be graduating from Bingham Academy the end of June, for it only went to grade nine. What would my future hold after that? Would I have to go back to Canada and, like my three older siblings, spend years without seeing Mom and Daddy and Sharilyn? My insides knotted at the thought. If I went to the American High School in Addis, how would I obtain a Canadian diploma? Would my folks consider letting me take correspondence like a couple of my friends had? There were many possibilities, ones which did not exist when my older siblings, Murray, Brian and Carolee, had finished Bingham. My head began to spin, so I dragged my mind back to the animated conversation and all Sharilyn's questions. *Today is too wonderful a day to spoil with these problems,* I thought.

We had three weeks until Christmas, – cloudless, dry-season days in the sunshine. I helped Mom around the house, dusting furniture, sweeping dirt into the wide cracks between our floorboards and ironing pretty embroidered pillowcases with heavy irons we heated on our cast-iron, wood-heated stove. Ato Bekulla and his wife, Lotwa, our neighbours, invited us for our favourite food – injera and wut. I often went across the compound to visit the Dyes and play with their little kids, whom I adored.

It was also fun to go talk to Daddy as he fixed the Land Rover. We always boasted at Bingham that our dad was the world's best mechanic. He would park the car under our huge fig tree. Then he'd attach ropes to the engine and loop them over one massive branch. Using the ropes and branch as a pulley system, he would pull the engine out. This let him work on the engine by itself, or he could slide under the car to fix the other parts. His hands and khaki clothes were covered with grease. But he always seemed to enjoy doing this kind of work.

When Auntie Fiona invited Sharilyn and me over for tea, we went, all dressed up and as pleased as duchesses to be served tea and cookies on china. I was eager to see if she had received any new books about the royal family from her British relatives. She hadn't, so I begged her to let me look, for the hundredth time, at her magazines of Princess Margaret's and Princess Alexandra's weddings.

We decorated a small, spindly pine tree in our living room and as Mom wrapped the gifts she'd made, or that Daddy had bought in Addis from her list, a little pile grew under the tree on the filing cabinet.

Mom and I listened to records on the record player, discussing our favourites, both classical and sacred music, and spent a lot of time whooping with laughter as we tried to figure out Julie Andrews' Cockney words in my new record, "My Fair Lady."

I told her about Grace Scheel, my latest piano teacher. "She's showing me how to play hymns like piano solos. I don't think I've ever enjoyed anything so much! Imagine, I get to play hymns during my practice time. You should hear the pretty things she's teaching me! She is giving me more and more difficult classical songs, too. I'm learning Chopin's Military Polonaise for graduation."

Mom clapped her hands. "Oh, I can hardly wait to hear you play it! I could listen to you all the time if we moved to Addis. It would be such a treat to live where there are pianos."

Before we knew it, Christmas Day had arrived. Sharilyn and I woke up early. Running into the living room, we found Daddy sitting in his pajamas on the couch, as he did every morning, wrapped in a blanket, praying.

"Daddy, can we open our stockings?" we begged, Sharilyn bouncing on the couch.

"Sure, go get Mom," he replied, stretching out his legs and yawning.

We ran into the bedroom, and caught Mom in the act of putting a bow on the final gift. "Mom, we want to open our stockings!"

"OK, I'll be right there."

Our stockings had been hung from nails on the rough mantel in the living room. I reached into the top of mine and pulled out a bottle of deodorant! *Oh groan,* I thought and grinned at Mom, rolling my eyes. Bingham had written on the lists they sent home with all the children that "older girls must bring deodorant," and I had complained how embarrassing it would be that everyone would read that.

Our stockings were filled with tangerines, nuts and candies and a little gift, too.

After that we crunched on our special, once-a-year breakfast treat – tiny boxes of Corn Flakes, Cheerios and Rice Krispies. Then we could open our presents. Mom had made Sharilyn and me each a new dress, just the right size and just the right colour. My eyes sparkled when I found out my next gift was a diary; I could hardly wait to write in it. Sharilyn squealed as she unwrapped a new doll.

That year, we had a great big Christmas dinner at our house with the other missionaries on the station and our Ethiopian neighbours. The men lugged in tables and chairs from each of the houses and benches from the elementary school, while the women cooked.

What a feast! Everyone lingered well into the afternoon, relaxing and visiting. The kids tore around in the house and outside, playing. When evening came, Mr. Dye turned on the generator and we sang carols by electric light, then read the Christmas story and visited some more. Finally, everyone lit their lanterns and walked across the compound to their homes.

Yawning but happy, Sharilyn and I crawled into bed, little shivers running down our spines at the sound of hyenas howling in the distance.

After Christmas, we still had another week and a half of holidays. I stood by Mom's sewing machine, watching her put final touches on our clothes, which were going into our suitcases. She had so much mending to do and also had to put our nametags on every single item - from our toothbrushes to our socks. While she worked, she told me beautiful things about the Lord, made crazy comments about life or composed goofy rhymes. I felt homesickness creeping over me already, so tried to concentrate on how I would enjoy showing my Bingham friends my pretty new dress and gifts.

In a few more days, a new term at boarding school would begin.

The day before we had to fly back to Addis, I slipped out of the house and went around the station. I strolled across the meadow and looked up at the Lambuda hills to the west, then gazed for a long time at the mountain panorama to the south. I sauntered down to the spring, from where a young boy would lead a donkey to our house every day, with tins of water on its back. In each special place, I recalled years of precious memories and said goodbye. I picked a couple of bougainvillea flowers, my favourites, and held them against my face, turned around to take one more look at beautiful Mount Shunkola then went back and sat in my bedroom, thinking.

I loved my unusual life in Ethiopia. It wasn't like the Ethiopians' lives and it wasn't like life in Canada but it was the best life I could imagine. I treasured these weeks we spent at home with our parents. I knew everything would soon change but that last day on Hosanna station, as I soaked in the sights, sounds and smells of the place that was dearer than any other place on earth to me, I knew it was a precious day I would never forget in Ethiopia, my home.

Chapter Two

—∞—

Called to Ethiopia

This story of my Ethiopian childhood actually begins six years before I was born. My parents, Manley and Mildred Hodges, lived with their two little boys, Murray and Brian, in Red Deer, Alberta, Canada, where they pastored a Baptist church.

In 1945, they felt that God was calling them to Ethiopia to be missionaries. Mom was only 23, Daddy 28, Murray was two and Brian almost a year old.

Mom was a marvellous storyteller and from the time I was very young, I would coax her to tell me about "the olden days." Watching her as she worked, going on a trip together and especially during the many times we looked through our family photo album, I would pester her with questions. Over the years, I learned more and more details and pieced her story together in my inquiring mind.

"In 1945, we were fresh out of Bible College and hardly knew a thing," reminisced Mom. "A lively missionary had come through Red Deer and preached at our church. She was having dinner with us and telling us stories about her work in Africa when she turned to us and exclaimed, 'You should become missionaries! You should! Africa is beginning to respond to the gospel and the Sudan Interior Mission is begging for missionaries to come help them in their work all across Africa.'"

"What did you say?" I asked.

"I had actually wanted to be a missionary when I was a child," Mom replied. "But that night when we went to bed we talked about it for a long time. Shortly afterwards, we met a man named Dr. Thompson. He had just come back from a trip to Ethiopia, where he had talked with the king and told us…"

"He knew King Haile Selassie?" I interrupted, my eyes opening wide.

"Yes, he did. He told us that Haile Selassie had asked for people to come to Ethiopia and help modernize his country. The emperor was calling for teachers, nurses, doctors, farmers - everyone. Dr. Thompson called it a 'wide open door for the gospel.'

"When he said that, we began to think seriously about going. We prayed about it a lot, then wrote to the mission's Canadian headquarters in Toronto, and asked them about it. They wrote right back, inviting us to apply. It takes most people a couple of years to get to the mission field after they apply but we were on our way to Ethiopia only about seven months later!"

"Why does it take most missionaries a long time?"

"Because they have to go for training with the mission in Toronto and they have to buy so many supplies to take to Africa. But the hardest thing to do is to raise support."

"What does that mean - raise support? And how come you didn't have a hard time doing it?"

"Raising support means finding people who will give money every month to help the missionaries live and work in Ethiopia. But Daddy and I both had families who loved the Lord. (Mom always referred to our dad as "Daddy" to us, so my sisters and I have called him "Daddy" all our lives.) Plus, our church in Red Deer belonged to a great organization that was very interested when we told them we wanted to go. We became their first missionaries."

"I thought you were the first missionaries of Bethel Baptist Church in Calgary."

"We were," answered Mom. "Bethel was the head church in the organization, much bigger than our little church in Red Deer. We talked to Bethel about wanting to go to Ethiopia and they were very happy with the idea of helping us. They agreed to send money to the mission for us each month. So between them and our families, we had all the support we needed quite quickly."

In 1945, the world did not know very much about Ethiopia. Many called it Abyssinia, a land of mystery. Even most of Africa knew hardly anything about Ethiopia, a kingdom of high, misty mountains that Africans could see from their hot, dry plains.

But that is where my parents felt God wanted them to go. So they found some boxes and barrels, shopped and packed up enough clothes and supplies to last them for five years. They said goodbye to their friends in Alberta and drove to see their families in Saskatchewan.

"That was the hard part," Mom told me. "Here we were going to an unknown country ten thousand miles away for five years!"

"Did they cry?" I asked.

"Yes, we all did but our families believed we were obeying God. They knew He would take care of us.

"So we drove all the way across Canada to the Toronto mission headquarters. We received our vaccinations and while waiting for our visas to come, we sent the boxes and barrels on ahead of us to Africa. When our visas arrived, we drove to New

York where we boarded a great big Swedish ocean liner called MS Gripsholm on October 16, 1945. A week later, while crossing the Atlantic Ocean, we celebrated Brian's first birthday.

"As we went from the Atlantic into the Mediterranean Sea, the Gripsholm had engine trouble. It limped along until it came to Italy, so we were put on a military ship, finally finishing our long ocean journey in Egypt. There we stayed in a houseboat on the Nile River."

I interjected, "You mean, you stayed on the actual Nile River?"

"Yes. The houseboat was our hotel. We could look out a little porthole and see the Nile River flowing by."

For many centuries, no one knew where the source of the Blue Nile River was. Explorers finally discovered it way up in the highlands of Ethiopia at a place called Lake Tana, which has a huge waterfall, the Blue Nile Falls. The Ethiopians called them "Tsississat" – "The smoky falls" – because the mist rising from the falls looked like smoke.

Egypt is mostly a desert, and the only place most of its people lived for thousands of years was along the Nile River. Thus, Egypt always had to depend on Ethiopia's rains to survive. It was truly a historic occasion for my parents to be staying on the Nile.

Mom continued, "A couple of days later, we stepped onto an Ethiopian Airlines airplane and headed for Addis Ababa, the capital of Ethiopia." She smiled at the memory. "We made one stop in Port Sudan, on the Red Sea. It was so hot, hotter than we'd ever experienced. It wasn't even cooler in the shade. When we took off again, we flew for hours over desert in Egypt and Sudan, until we noticed the land under us beginning to change to green hills and mountains. The mountains went higher and higher up. It was beautiful. When we landed in Addis Ababa, and walked down the steps of the airplane, we were thrilled to find that the air was cool!"

I smiled at that. Almost everyone thinks that all of Africa is very hot but in Ethiopia, even when the sun shines brightly and there are no clouds in the sky, the weather is not hot at all. Ethiopia is a mountainous country on a high plateau – called "the highlands" – with altitudes from 5000 to 10,000 feet above sea level, making the weather very pleasant.

Mom proceeded with her story. "A few weeks after arriving in Addis, we received a message saying that our boxes had arrived, and we could go pick them up. We were so relieved because we wouldn't have to live out of our suitcases any more. But when the boxes finally arrived, they were in terrible condition. The sides were ripped, the top edges caved in, lids pried open."

"What on earth happened?" I asked.

"We realized that people who worked at the ports along the Red Sea had gone through our stuff and taken almost everything. My wedding china and..."

"Your wedding china!" I exclaimed, knowing how much my mother loved pretty china.

"Yes, even my wedding dress was gone."

"Oh, Mom, your wedding dress! The one Grandma made for you?"

"Yes," she replied, "I especially loved it because my mom had sewn it. To this day, I've always pictured an Arab lady walking down a dusty desert trail, wearing my wedding dress. Sigh."

"What did you do?" I asked. "Did the market even have kids' clothes and stuff for your house in those days?" When I

14

lived in Addis, the huge market had so many things but Mom and Daddy came in 1945, which seemed like centuries before.

"Mm-hmm. The missionaries were really wonderful. They gave us linens from what little they had because you couldn't get towels and sheets in Ethiopia. We went to the market and actually had fun picking out material and clothes for the boys and ourselves. We couldn't afford too many things but it was a start. We also found some kitchen items – plates, a tin kettle, a broom."

"Daddy gave me a big hug and said, 'Don't worry, Mil. The Lord led us to come here and He knew this would happen. He'll take care of us.' That cheered me up. I had begun to see that missionary life was quite an adventure."

"You've always loved adventure," I raved. "I think you're the perfect missionary!"

Mom grinned and patted my cheek. "Yes, I sure do love it!"

My parents' mission was called Sudan Interior Mission. Three young men had started it in 1893. Rowland Bingham, Thomas Kent and Walter Gowans went to Africa to preach the gospel in an area called "Soudan," that stretched all across Africa, just south of the great Sahara Desert. In those days Africa was called "the white man's grave" because so many of them died there of malaria. Very soon, Kent and Gowans died of malaria. Only Rowland Bingham lived and went on to establish the Sudan Interior Mission. Over 50 years later, when Mom and Daddy first went to Africa, the mission had spread to Ethiopia.

Ethiopia is a land of mountains, rivers, hills and forests of fragrant eucalyptus trees. In 1945, there were hardly any roads, except a few that the Italians had built when they occupied Ethiopia for five years during the Second World War.

The people of Ethiopia speak a language called Amharic. As soon as my parents arrived, the Mission Director told them that the first thing they needed to do was learn the language. They immediately began to memorize the big alphabet of about 250 letters. Mom always said that when they finally learned the alphabet, it was easy to read the language because it was completely phonetic – it sounded exactly the way it looked.

Not long afterwards, the mission asked them to move south to the province of Kaffa. Kaffa is famous because coffee was discovered there over a thousand years ago. In fact, the word "coffee" comes from "Kaffa." The story is told of a young Ethiopian goatherd who noticed that when his goats ate certain little red beans on bushes, they were much more frisky and sometimes stayed awake all night. Goats always seemed to me to be a complete nuisance anyway because they eat almost anything. They will chew on your shoes, your toys, even sometimes poisonous plants like poinsettias, instead of just eating grass nicely like sheep.

Gradually Ethiopians found that if they roasted these beans, they turned dark brown and gave off a pleasant aroma. One day someone must have ground those roasted beans, boiled them and thought it made a nice-tasting drink because it became more and more popular until many people were drinking this new brew and calling it "coffee."

But before the mission asked my parents to move, something exciting happened – a new little one joined their family. On January 22, 1946, Vernon Barry was born in Addis Ababa. The Hodges now had three little boys. So in April 1946, my parents, with Murray, Brian and baby Vernon, packed all their things into a great big old Italian truck that was heading down to Kaffa. Two other Canadian ladies, Jean Paton, a nurse, and Beverly Macomber, a teacher, went with them.

"The roads were bumpy," Mom said, never tiring of telling this part of the story. "The trip took days but the scenery was absolutely breathtaking! All along the way we saw monkeys and many different kinds of birds. Beside the road wrecked tanks and guns lay about, stripped of everything that was valuable. They were weapons left from the war when the British drove out the Italians.

"We drove down, miles down, into the great Omo River gorge and crossed the river on a narrow bridge. Looking out the truck windows, we could see crocodiles and hippos on the banks. Our truck groaned as it slowly climbed back up the other side."

Mom's eyes filled with wonder as she gestured with her hands. "Valleys, plateaus and mountain ranges stretched beyond us as far as the eye could see. I kept exclaiming, 'Oh, have you ever seen anything like this! Look at those vistas!' I knew Ethiopia was a pretty country but I had absolutely no idea it was so gorgeous! The weather became warmer, because the altitude was lower than Addis and the country was lush and green. We finally arrived at a small city called Jimma, the capital of Kaffa."

"But Jimma wasn't the end of your journey."

"Nope," Mom replied. "We still had to go farther on to Agaro. It seemed like the end of the world. We drove through forests, on bumpy dirt roads, up steep hills, taking sharp turns. We had to cross streams which had no bridges."

I knew that in the rainy season, neither car nor truck could ever drive through because the roads would be so muddy. Both Ethiopians and missionaries would have to ride mules and donkeys instead. But this was the end of the dry season so Mom and Daddy and the two ladies could still go by truck.

17

"Finally," Mom said, "we arrived at a beautiful mission station in the midst of a forest. We saw a wide, clear space in front of a house with a tin roof, a hedge of roses all around it, and flowers at one side. And, oh, the trees! There were banana trees, papaya trees, a guava orchard, and as always, the tall, swaying eucalyptus trees. It was a wild, unkempt place but just gorgeous. We walked around, gazing in awe at where we would be living.

"We soon realized that Jean and Beverly would have to live with us in the little two-bedroom house until Daddy could build them a house of their own. Jean would begin holding a clinic under a tree to give out medicine and treat sick people. Beverly was going to teach at a government school in Agaro town."

"Wasn't she the one Brian called 'Auntie Bubberly?'" I asked, giggling.

"Yes, that's right. Auntie Bubberly."

"Weren't you glad someone had built a mission house at Agaro?"

"Yes, the mission had started a work there before the war and built this house. It had two bedrooms, a living/dining room, a kitchen and a small bathroom."

I wrinkled up my nose. "But the toilet was outside."

"Yes, of course. The toilets are always outside," Mom replied, jabbing me with her elbow.

"We began to unpack our suitcases and boxes, and set up the house. Like all the mission houses, it was built of very thick mud walls and had plenty of windows but without glass or shutters. No one had lived in it for a few years and it was a terrible mess. Goats had wandered in and out and left plenty of evidence of having been there. It was overrun with rats and the floor was full of jiggers."

Oh, I knew all about jiggers! They were little tiny black insects that got into your feet, if you went barefoot, and laid a sack of eggs. Fortunately, Ethiopians knew how to fish the egg sack out without breaking it, using a large, blunt safety pin.

Mom went on, "So everyone went after the rats, cleaned the whole place out, and put DDT all over the floor. *That* fixed the jiggers!" (DDT was a powder used a lot in those days to kill bugs. Eventually most governments banned it because it is very harmful to people as well.)

"For the first few days, as our family and the two ladies stumbled around and over boxes piled everywhere, it rained nearly every day. It seemed like we were bringing more mud into the house than we could clean. On the third day, we put our stove up, and moved in a kitchen cabinet Daddy had made. Until then we had been cooking on a small, one-burner kerosene stove.

Jean Paton had brought a metal wardrobe and Daddy got the bright idea of putting shelves in it so we could use it for storing food. Ha, ha! The rats could not chew through the metal and eat our food!

"The mission had given us the stove and beds and we found bamboo chairs and wooden tables in the Agaro market. We set up our beds right away, of course, and found our lamps in the boxes."

I nodded, knowing how important it would be to find those lamps. Night falls suddenly in Africa, and except for nights when the moon is full, it becomes dark quickly, with no twilight. I asked, "Wasn't it scary to go to bed at night with no glass in the windows, hearing the sounds of hyenas, monkeys, leopards and birds?"

"Yes, one of the first things Daddy did was make shutters

for the windows. We left the shutters open in the day but pulled them closed at night and latched them on hooks in the windowsill."

Mom went on to tell me that she had to shoot a monkey more than once because they kept trying to come into the house to steal bananas. She called them "real saucy little pests." When my mom was young, her father had taught all his children to use a gun and handle it carefully, so she had brought a gun with her and quickly put it to good use. She would hang the dead monkey in the orchard as a lesson to the other monkeys. But always its carcass disappeared by the morning. She figured a hungry hyena removed it and had a free feast.

"Right from the start people came to visit us. We discovered it was an Ethiopian custom to call on someone new. The people were very friendly. A young man came in wanting to be our cook. We liked him very much. We also hired a good houseboy who served the table, washed dishes and helped clean the house. Then we hired a laundry boy who spent his time singing goofy songs. He didn't get the clothes clean, and couldn't iron but he was a great entertainer.

"We discovered that the people around Agaro were mostly Moslems, people who could only be won over by house-to-house visiting, so we tried to set up house quickly, so we could go out among them and take our kids too. The people loved the children, and hugged and kissed them as much as they could before the boys protested."

Mom had a far-away look, remembering those long-ago days. She concluded, "Soon life began to feel normal and oh, how spoiled we felt to be able to live in such a beautiful place! A missionary visiting us once joked that the grass grew so fast that if you stood too long in one place, it would grow up around your feet! I wrote to my family, 'How happy we are to be here, and we love every bit of it!'"

Chapter Three

—∞—

Life at Beautiful Agaro

I asked Daddy how they learned Amharic. He told me that when he and Mom first used to visit their neighbours at Agaro, they took little notebooks with them. They would point to an object and ask, "Mindino? – What is that?" – a phrase they had already learned in Addis Ababa. Then they would write down the answer in their notebooks and practise saying the words.

Murray and Brian, on the other hand, quickly made friends with the little neighbour boys and learned to speak Amharic right away, since children learn languages fast. Mom would call them for dinner and they would run into the house, chattering to each other in Amharic. Soon even Mom and Daddy started asking them for help with words or phrases.

Mom became friends with a woman named Balainish, whose husband was the governor of Agaro. Balainish had moved from Gondar, an ancient city of the Amhara tribe in northern Ethiopia, so she spoke perfect Amharic. Mom said, "I learned a lot from her. I sat in her house on a little three-legged stool and watched her cook injera and wut. I got to taste some of it too! She was such a gracious lady and we soon became the best of friends."

Mom practised long and hard, listening to Balainish, imitating her as she spoke, carefully pronouncing her words. She really enjoyed language lessons and she and Daddy learned Amharic better and better during their first couple of years in

Ethiopia. Over the years, they both became very fluent. In fact, eventually, Mom could speak Amharic so well that Ethiopians said that if they weren't looking when she was speaking with a group of Ethiopians, they could not tell who was not the Ethiopian.

Above all else, Mom's and Daddy's passion was for the people of Kaffa to hear about Jesus. Even as young Christians in their twenties, they had learned the value of prayer. Over and over they fasted, day after day they prayed. They and the other two missionaries spent so much time in prayer and fasted so often, they began to see quite a few people become saved. This was amazing because Agaro was an area, which was traditionally known as being "hard to reach with the gospel."

Gradually, as their Amharic improved, they were better able to share the good news. Almost every day, they walked the roads, visiting their neighbours, stopping in the market to chat with the vendors, not only in Agaro town but also the surrounding villages. They invited the people they met to come to the church services they started holding on Sunday. Many did come out of curiosity.

Mom began to hold children's classes. She cut out flannel pictures that her family had sent from Canada. She painted backgrounds on flannel cloth to put the pictures on, so she could tell Bible stories. Children loved to hear the stories and as they went home they would sing the new songs they had learned. Soon many of them responded to the gospel and gave their hearts to Jesus.

Every day Daddy went down to the clinic where people were standing in line and started talking to them about Jesus. He was a wonderful storyteller and the people soon forgot how long they were waiting as they listened to him. Day after day, many of them became believers.

One of their kitchen workers had a wife who was badly oppressed by demons. Mom and Daddy had never seen anything like this but they had read about it in the Bible. So they fasted and prayed together for several days. When they laid hands on her and prayed for her, she was delivered! How happy they were that by obeying what they read in the Bible, they could actually see God bring peace to this tormented woman. The townspeople took notice too. Slowly, they began to come to Jesus – two or three travellers on the road here, a neighbour lady there, children in the daily Bible class and many at the clinic. Whenever it seemed that not as many were being saved, the missionaries fasted and prayed. Time and again they found that as they did this, more would be saved in their services and in their daily contacts.

All this time Mom cared for her little boys, cooked, sewed and wrote letters to friends and family in Canada. Daddy built a clinic and a school and worked in and around the station. Sometimes he rode a mule to Jimma for business to pick up the mail and supplies. He would stop to visit with people he saw along the way, and always he would end up telling them the good news of salvation.

On one of his many trips to Jimma, Daddy met Vergari, an Italian man who lived in Jimma (the capital of Kaffa, about seventeen miles from Agaro), and he became good friends with Mom and Daddy. Vergari had a big, old white Ardita car, and sometimes Daddy would ride between Jimma and Agaro with him. Once they even drove as far as Addis. Daddy said, "He was always happy to see us when we came to visit but he refused to learn any English. He said Italian was the most beautiful language in the world so he taught it to us."

"But we didn't mind and we learned a lot of phrases," added Mom, "because Italian is supposed to be the easiest language to learn." Vergari came to Ethiopia during the Second World War. He liked it so much that he stayed. When Emperor Haile Selassie came back after the British drove out the Italian army, he told his people to forgive the Italians and let them stay if they wanted to. So Vergari settled in the lush area of Kaffa. He invited the Hodges to his place or visited them in their home. He enjoyed the children and would hold the babies and pat their soft tummies, saying, "*Bello poncholino*," which is Italian for "beautiful tummy."

My parents also met a Greek mill owner in Agaro. He could not speak English either. He did speak Amharic, though, so Mom and Daddy could easily talk with him. The Ethiopians looked at them in amazement, laughing behind their hands. They thought it was so funny to watch these three white people talk to each other in Amharic.

In January 1947, Murray and Brian started coughing all the time and were very tired. They stopped playing with their friends and did not feel like eating. Soon they started coughing up blood and Mom and Daddy decided they needed to take them to Addis. The doctor said it was tuberculosis, a serious disease that killed many people in those days. He suggested they go to Harar, a hot and dry town far away, which had a tuberculosis hospital. Other people said they would have to go home to Canada. Mom said, "We felt so badly at the thought of having to leave Agaro, all the friends we had made there and the little church we had started. So we did the only thing we knew to do – we got down on our knees and prayed. And God answered our prayers. One of the senior missionaries, a dear Scotsman, asked if he could anoint the boys with oil and pray for them, according to the Bible verse, James 5:16. He told us his church in Scotland had that practice. We readily agreed.

"So he came and anointed Murray and Brian with oil and prayed for them. Almost immediately they stopped coughing. They began to eat everything on their plates again and even asked for seconds. They started running around the apartment and asking when they could go outside and play. They were healed! We were just thrilled to have our boys healthy again. And now we could go back home to Agaro."

With Murray, Brian & Vernon at Agaro

A few months later, little Vernon became very sick. It was

in June, the rainy season, and it was impossible to travel on the terrible, muddy roads. Worst of all, the nurse was away. Vernon did not want to eat anything because his throat was so sore. He lay quite still in his bed.

The next morning he woke up with a croupy cough and his voice was completely gone. Mom and Daddy tried to help him in every way they knew, and stayed up almost all night rubbing compresses on him, putting a tent over his crib and boiling camphor steam into it so he could breathe better. He could hardly breathe and didn't seem aware of anything going on around him.

The following day about noon his skin turned a greyish colour and he was so weak. In the afternoon, Mom and Daddy knelt at his bedside to pray, anointed their precious little boy with oil and committed him to the Lord. They took turns carrying him around. Finally, he took a long breath and slipped away to be with Jesus. It was June 11, 1947.

Mom and Daddy knew their baby had gone to heaven but they had never experienced such pain and sorrow. That first night after Vernon died, they hardly slept, pacing the little house, weeping and holding each other, knowing they would never see their little boy again on this earth.

Mom dressed him the next morning in a little suit, the kind where the top buttons onto the pants. Daddy made a tiny coffin out of cedar wood; they put soft padding in it and laid him in it, spreading over his small white body a finely-woven Ethiopian shawl. With tears pouring down her cheeks, Mom wrote a poem, while sobbing so hard she could barely see what she was writing:

> Oh little one, so sweet and fair, like a faded flower there,
> My little boy with curly hair.

27

Oh little one, so still and cold, gathered so soon to Jesus'
fold,
Just sixteen and a half months old.
And yet, not here, my baby sweet but playing at the
Saviour's feet,
Where all of us, again, shall meet.

Neighbours and friends streamed into their house all day to
offer sympathy and help. They knew how it felt to lose a baby
because there was hardly a home where a child had not died.
Several men dug a grave, in the shadow of the forest. That
afternoon, two men carried the little coffin out to the graveside,
draped with a sheet, and covered with roses. And as everybody
gathered around, Daddy told them that he and his family would
see their baby again in heaven. He pleaded with them to believe
in Jesus so they could have this hope too.

A few months later, when they talked about Vernon's death
with a doctor in Jimma, he told them that he had died of croup,
which is like diphtheria. He also told them that if he had been
there, he could have made a simple incision in Vernon's neck so
he could breathe and his life probably would have been spared.
Oh, how heartbreaking was that thought!

Over the next few weeks, my mom wrote poems, trying to
heal the hurt in her heart:

I think of the lonesome days ahead, with the little voice
quite still
Of the empty chair and the empty bed, and the toys on
the windowsill.
Of the little shoes, with no wee feet, to run with them at
play,
And the little clothes laid clean and neat, untouched from
day to day.

Of the surging joy that was ours before, just to see his dear wee face,

And the laughter we shall hear no more for he's gone from his little place.

For the voice has ceased and the sun gone down on the forest, the home, and the heart.

In the desolateness, in the twilight gloom, is there none to bear a part?

Yes, there is One who can understand, and in the midst of grief bring joy,

Because, for us, in that shining land, He is keeping our little boy.

She wrote this poem in July 1947, so full of meaning to anyone who has ever lived in Ethiopia:

The Little Grave

On Ethiopia's wooded hills the rain is falling down,

Thin, filmy mists of sweeping rain, on forest, field and town.

And many rains have fallen, yet two moons the skies will weep

Upon the little, new-made grave, the forest by, asleep.

Yet two months and the yellow flowers, September's carpeting

Upon each grassy slope will bloom, and boys and girls will sing

The age-old "Muskel" songs; but still the little grave will lie

Through Ethiopia's seasons, beneath her summer sky.

The stately birds sail over, the little birds flit near,

The monkeys leaping through the trees know not that it

is here.

The dusky Kaffa farmer, to his labors goes apace
Down the shadowed forest path, nor knows its little place.
And Ethiopia's summers, and her rains will come and go
But all this mother's heart thoughts, only her God can know,
And each unsounded depth of pain, and every tear that fell,
And in her grief speak comfort, He will assure her, "It is well."

For days, the neighbours crowded their home and sat with them. Sometimes they brought food or drink but usually came just to sit and show they cared. They felt the Hodges were now like so many of them who had also lost children. Mom and Daddy appreciated their comfort so much, because they knew that their lives must go on in spite of their tragedy.

Back in Canada, their families grieved with them too. Uncle Ken said Grandpa Hodges wept as he read their letter, something he had never seen him do before.

"Soon," Mom told me, "I began to long for another baby. My first three babies had been born close together, so I expected to become pregnant quickly but many months went by. It wasn't until almost a year later that I found that I was going to have another baby! I knew this baby was a gift from God to comfort us. I really hoped we would have a girl."

In December 1948, the family drove to Addis Ababa to wait for the new arrival. Three days after Christmas, Mom went to the Seventh Day Adventist Hospital (called "Fill Wooha" Hospital, or "Boiling Water" Hospital) and gave birth to a beautiful little girl. They named her Carolee Rose. Finally joy

began to replace the ache of losing Vernon.

When Mom was able to make the long trip back to Agaro with her little girl, neighbours and townspeople crowded around, touching and asking to hold her. Ethiopians have very dark brown eyes, and they exclaimed about the white man's children with their blue eyes. They looked up at them, declaring that Carolee, like Mom and Brian, had "cat's eyes." (Daddy's and Murray's eyes were hazel-coloured.)

The whole family loved to play with their new little girl. Murray and Brian called Carolee "Sweetie." I think they thought it was her name because they heard Mom and Daddy call her that so often.

One day Mary Thornton, the new station nurse, brought some shocking news. Someone had abandoned a baby girl at the clinic. Even though they inquired all over town, no one knew whose baby she was. Mom and Daddy talked for a long time that night, and by morning came to a decision: they would adopt her. Daddy went into Agaro the very next morning to apply for permission and fill out the necessary papers. And little Fikiray, a sweet Ethiopian name that means "My Love," came home to live with the Hodges. But Fikiray was very sick and lived only a few days. So Daddy dug another small grave and placed her beside Vernon.

In just a few months, Mom was surprised to discover that

she was pregnant again! Carolee was five months old, barely able to sit up but as the rainy season progressed, Mom's tummy grew large faster than in any previous pregnancy.

In August, Mom was busy with work around the station and continued to fast with the others who were praying for revival. Then her blood pressure started going higher and she began to have stomach pains. She realized she needed to slow down in order to keep her baby. She said, "I decided to stay in bed so Carolee could have a little sister." It worked and she started feeling much better.

But on September 27th, 1949, she did go into labour. It was far too early for the baby to be born, and the nurse was away again, so Daddy gave her morphine. He got everything ready as Mom's labour pains progressed, and she delivered a tiny girl. But no sooner was that little girl born than another one began to be born! Mom was having twins! But because they were four months early, they did not live. Today, with technologically advanced equipment in hospitals, doctors can save premature babies' lives but on a far-away mission station in 1949, where there was no hospital and not even a nurse, there was nothing they could do for the twins. How sad they were and grieved and wept over this painful loss! They were so looking forward to a new little sister for Carolee, Murray and Brian but now they had lost two little sisters.

Mom and Daddy lined a shoebox with some soft fabric and laid the little girls in it. Mom said they looked like china dolls; their skin was so white.

A white, double cross for the twins' grave now joined the single crosses over Vernon's and Fikiray's graves.

Once again, friends, neighbours and believers came to sit with them and comfort them. Once again they listened as the white man told them his two little girls had gone to heaven and had joined their son and Fikiray with Jesus. Again they nodded and murmured as he explained to them how to believe so they could have the same hope.

Even though the twins didn't live, Mom and Daddy still thought they should have names. Mom had always disliked her name, Mildred, and she had wished her whole childhood that she had been named Kathleen. So they called one of the twins Kathleen and the other Karen because the two names seemed to go together so perfectly.

Chapter Four

—∞—

Murray Goes To Boarding School

The Hodges' small house was crowded because the two Canadian missionary ladies were still living with them and their three children in a two-bedroom house. Murray and Brian called the ladies "Auntie Beverley" and "Auntie Mary." Mom and Daddy often referred to them as "the girls."

So Daddy built a new house for "the girls." But he didn't design one like his own house, rectangular and with a tin roof. Instead, he decided to build it like the Ethiopian houses – round, and with a thatched roof. Unlike their houses, he would add glass windows and hinged doors.

First he bought sturdy poles then he dug holes in a circle to put the poles in. He wove strips of a rope-like plant called "inset" between the poles to keep them steady. This formed the outside wall of the house.

Curious about this white man building a home like theirs, men from the community came to help him. They made a wide, shallow pit where they trampled mud, mixing it with straw, singing as they trudged round and round. They took the mud and plastered the round wall Daddy had constructed. Mud made nice, smooth walls, keeping the coolness in and the heat out and the straw kept the mud from falling apart after it dried. It was a very practical building material for homes built in Ethiopia.

When it came time to put on the pointed thatched roof, the

34

Ethiopians looked around for a tall, thick, strong centre pole to hold up the roof just like they all used in their own houses. They were puzzled and even worried when Daddy said he didn't need one. He knew that the structure of the building he had made would hold the roof without a centre pole. The Ethiopians were sure the roof would fall in. Much to their surprise, it did not. Later, Mom made a ceiling out of a thin cheesecloth material, which kept bugs from falling out of the thatched roof onto the missionaries' things.

So Auntie Beverly Macomber and Auntie Mary Thornton moved in and set up their own place. Miss Macomber now taught school on the station instead of in town and Miss Thornton was able to treat people in the clinic Daddy had built.

Every now and then a big Italian truck would come to Agaro. These trucks were called *"trente quatros."* It was so unusual to see a vehicle on the station that for days afterwards Murray and Brian played "trucks" with everything they could find, making truck noises with their mouths. Once an airplane had to make a forced landing in a meadow near the town. Our family and the whole town ran out to see the plane. It stayed there for almost a month before it was fixed. After that everything was "airplanes" for the boys. At mealtime, they crossed their forks over their knives and flew them through the air. For days they pretended they were pilots.

Dry season lasted until about April, when light rains began to fall. In June, July and August the heavy rains came. It rained and rained and rained, and everything became greener and greener. The boys had to wear boots when they played outside. Sometimes it drizzled for days and they had to play inside. How boring! The sun would come out for a while but before long it would rain again. All of Ethiopia seemed to stand still during the rainy season. It was too difficult to travel through the thick mud, so people simply stayed home.

Beautiful Agaro station. Our house is to the right. See the round house Daddy built? Just beyond that is the school and peeking over the top of our house is the roof of the clinic.

Suddenly, in mid-September, little yellow Muskel flowers came out and covered the land. Winds blew and the rains stopped. Then for months, hardly a drop of rain fell because it was dry season.

By Christmastime, the grass had turned brown; but the weather was so nice and warm, nobody minded. Little Carolee, "Sweetie," was a good baby and the whole family lavished love on her. She was learning to take steps. She celebrated her first Christmas and then her first birthday three days later.

At the end of February, my mom started to get Murray ready to go to boarding school in Addis, sewing him clothes and filling his suitcase. She always said, "The hardest part of missionary life *by far* was having to send you kids away to

36

school. But it was much worse in the years before we came to Ethiopia, so we sure didn't want to complain. Missionaries used to have to leave their children back in Canada, not seeing them for five whole years, because there was no school in Ethiopia for them. But in 1946 God called an American couple, Mr. and Mrs. Hay, and told them to start a school in Addis for missionaries' children. Oh, it was sure a lot easier to be away from you kids for only nine months, rather than having to leave you for five years. What a blessing the Hays were to the mission!"

The school year began in March and ended in December. How my parents dreaded sending six-year-old Murray so far away and not seeing him for nine months. But the day did come. On Mom's birthday, March 8th, 1950, Mom hugged Murray with all her might. Brian cried as he said goodbye, thinking how lonesome he would be for his brother.

As Daddy and Murray took off down the road together to make the long trip to Addis, Mom held Brian and Carolee close to her, swallowing a great big lump in her throat. Later, alone in her bedroom, she sat down and sobbed. However, there was still much to do, so she wiped away her tears, got back to work, and waited for the day Daddy would come back.

Daddy and Murray rode some mules to Jimma then took a truck to Addis. When they arrived in Addis, Daddy took Murray to the School for Missionaries' Children (SMC), where they talked to Mr. and Mrs. Hay but then it was time to say goodbye.

Murray did not want to let go of his dad but Daddy had to go, so he bent down to give him a big, long hug. Then he went out the gate and down the road. The watchman closed the gate behind him. Murray ran to the gate, climbed up onto a railing, reached his arms through the bars, crying as though his heart would break. Daddy had to keep on walking, his heart aching. Murray begged for him to come back but Daddy knew he could not. That night at the mission headquarters, Daddy hardly slept, thinking of Murray. Over and over, he pictured him crying at the gate and tears ran from his eyes, falling onto his pillow. He promised himself that he would not tell my mom how terrible it had been to leave their little boy. She would not be able bear it. He did not tell her for many years.

The Hays wrote to Daddy and Mom often, saying that Murray was starting to fit in and play with the other children. At first he stayed mostly to himself but gradually he became used being away from his parents, just like all the other kids. The Hays were kind and understanding.

Murray made good friends with boys like Howie Brant, Van Schmidt, Denny Hoekstra, Bobby Ratzliff and others. Soon he was doing well. When Mom and Daddy sent him letters, a member of the staff read them to him. He grew thoughtful as though he were imagining his family far away. My parents wrote cheerful letters and asked him lots of questions so he would not feel homesick. Every week he sat with one of the older boys who helped him write a letter back to them. He was becoming accustomed to boarding school life.

Back at Agaro, my parents discovered the amazing grace of God, which helps us go through difficult times. Although they never did stop missing Murray, the painful hurt slowly went away. They knew they were called to take the gospel to people who had never heard of Jesus and that being a missionary meant going through difficult times. So they accepted the fact and thanked God that He always helped them through their pain. Hundreds of people did come to know Jesus and their lives were forever changed. Up in heaven, I know God smiled as He prepared a big, eternal reward for my mom and dad.

Many years later, Mom told me, "Every now and then, for just a few seconds, it was as though the Lord pulled back a curtain and I was filled with the most unbearable pain and loneliness. Then, just as quickly, the curtain closed and I felt His grace wash over me, and the pain went away. I believe God wanted me to know the grief and hurt His grace was keeping me from. I was overcome with gratefulness."

That year, Brian and Carolee played together a lot. They ran around in the sun together. Mom made them wear little helmets, so they wouldn't get sunburned. She even put a net on the helmets, so flies and mosquitoes couldn't land on their faces.

Brian started going to Miss Macomber's school with his Ethiopian friends, where he learned both the Amharic and English alphabet. Soon he was learning to read, something he would love to do all his life. This gave him a head start for when he eventually did start first grade.

In May, Mom became pregnant again. The Hodges family had been in Ethiopia for almost five years. They had experienced such happiness, along with deep sadness. After five years, they would be allowed to go back to Canada for a year. This baby would be born in Canada.

Finally the time arrived that they could pack up to leave on furlough. In November 1950, they said goodbye to the Agaro missionaries, staff, believers and all the friends they had made and found a truck to take them to Addis.

When they reached Addis, the whole family immediately took a taxi to the School for Missionaries' Children to see Murray. Whenever Mom told me about it, she had to blink back her tears. "We were so excited. When we arrived at SMC, we went to find Murray. When he saw us, the look on his face was absolute astonishment. It was as though he had thought he would never see us again. We hugged and laughed, cried and hugged some more. Murray did not stop smiling the rest of the day."

As the oldest child in our family, Murray made it much easier for his brother and sisters when we had to go to boarding school. None of us Hodges children would ever have as hard a time as he had. We would each always have another sibling at school.

The Hodges did not go back to Agaro but stayed in Addis for the next three weeks, preparing to go to Canada. Mom was seven months pregnant and went to the mission doctor for a check-up. He took her blood pressure and discovered it was 190 over 140! He pointed his finger at her and said, "You get home to Canada right now! And no more babies after this one!"

In a few days they flew to Aden where they found a ship, a Norwegian freighter, to take them back home to Canada. What fun the boys had, exploring all over the ship but Mom suffered from seasickness the whole way. After eighteen days the ship docked in the big port of Boston in the U.S.A. Brian and Murray were excited to see black men helping unload the big ship and ran to speak Amharic to them. The men looked at them with puzzled faces and didn't answer. They had no idea what Murray and Brian were saying, because they were not Ethiopians, they were Americans!

From Boston, the Hodges took a train to New York and then up to Toronto, Canada. It was December and the boys were thrilled to see snow but as the train chugged west across the country, and all they saw outside the window was snow, snow, and more snow, it became very dreary.

When they finally reached their families in Saskatchewan, everyone was so happy to see them. What a grand reunion they had with parents, brothers and sisters! Then they continued on to Calgary, Alberta and settled down to enjoy a wonderful year together as a family.

Can you guess who the little baby was that would soon be born in Canada?

Chapter Five

—∞—

The Hodges' First Furlough

Furlough was such an exciting time!

Murray and Brian did not remember anything about Canada because they had been so young when they had left. It was completely different from what they were used to in Ethiopia – everything was so big and modern. Carolee had never seen Canada but at two years old, she didn't notice much anyway.

My mom's and dad's families wanted to know all about what life was like in Africa. It was wonderful to be able to have long visits. They sat around talking, laughing, crying, showing pictures, asking and answering many questions. Everyone basked in the luxury of visiting for days with those they loved and had missed so much. Many things change in five years.

For one thing, Daddy's brothers and some of Mom's siblings had married and started having children of their own. Murray, Brian and Carolee had six new cousins; Murray and Brian were the oldest of all the cousins.

Daddy's family were the Hodges. Grandma Hodges was from England and Grandpa Hodges was from Wales. They had come to Canada, married and travelled west to start a farm in Saskatchewan near a town called Wiseton. That is where Daddy and his two younger brothers, Ernie and Ken, grew up. Sadly, Grandpa died of cancer on October 16, 1947. Mom and Daddy were in Agaro at the time and it took a whole month for the news to reach them.

Daddy's brother, Ernie, went to Prairie Bible Institute in Three Hills, Alberta, where he met his future wife, Jean. The Bible Institute strongly encouraged students to become missionaries, so Uncle Ernie applied to the Sudan Interior Mission – Mom and Daddy's mission – to work in Nigeria. Aunt Jean applied to go to Nigeria, too. The mission accepted both of them but asked them to wait a bit before getting married, so they went to Africa as single people in 1946.

When Uncle Ernie and Aunt Jean married in Nigeria on June 30th, 1948, Uncle Ken and Aunt Margaret had their wedding on exactly the same day back home in Saskatchewan. They planned it that way because that was Mom and Daddy's anniversary, so all three Hodges brothers had the same wedding anniversary. (On that very day, Mom had to be in Addis for medical treatment. She wrote about it saying, "...our 6th anniversary, with 245 miles of Ethiopia's rainy-season mud between us!")

Since Nigeria was so hot, Uncle Ernie and Aunt Jean only had to stay for four-year terms. That meant they came home on furlough the same year as our family. They now had a little boy, David, and a baby, Ruthie. What a blessing it was to compare their missionary lives in the two countries across the continent of Africa from each other. Daddy and Uncle Ernie even travelled for six weeks together to Bible Schools all over the Canadian prairies. They had pictures on transparent slides that they could put in front of a light and shine on a big screen for all the Bible students to see. As they described their lives in Africa, they were able to help the students realize how thrilling it was to bring the good news to people who had never heard of or experienced God's love.

In later years, whenever Daddy looked back on this time

with his brother, he realized how special it had been because once they went back to Africa, Daddy never saw him again. In 1953, Daddy received a telegram from Nigeria saying that Uncle Ernie had died suddenly of polio on November 22nd. He had been sick for only four days before dying. What a terrible shock! They had three little children, David, Ruthie and Danny and were expecting their fourth child. Dear Aunt Jean was going to have to raise those children without her husband, the love of her life. Her fourth baby was born a little over a month later on New Year's Day, 1954 and she named him Ernest John after his father.

Aunt Jean decided not to go back to Canada but to stay and teach at Kent Academy, the school for missionaries' children in Nigeria. It was named for Thomas Kent, one of the three men who started the Sudan Interior Mission. For over twenty years, many missionaries' kids would have our Aunt Jean for their teacher. I always thought she was one of the sweetest ladies I knew. Living at the school, she was able to be with all her kids as they grew up in Nigeria.

Uncle Ken, Daddy's youngest brother, decided not to be a missionary. He believed that God wanted him to stay home in Canada and look after their mom who was left alone after Grandpa died. In 1950, he moved a little house for her next door to his family's house in Wiseton, where he and Aunt Margaret could lovingly watch over her. She lived there for many years until she died in 1984 at the age of 95.

My mom's family, the Dewars, was a real "cowboy" family. Grandpa Dewar and Mom's two brothers, Gordon and Donny, had competed in many rodeos, including the famous Calgary Stampede. But it was Uncle Donny Dewar who made rodeo a career. He rode in rodeos all across Canada and the U.S., travelling with his wife and kids in a trailer. He won awards as a world champion bronc rider and bulldogger. In fact, a picture of him on a bucking bronco hung in the Calgary Stampede's main building for many years.

My mom and her siblings had all learned to ride horses as soon as they could walk. Her two sisters, Claire and Lois, spent every spare minute they could on horses and began to teach themselves how to do tricks on them. One day, when Uncle Donny was visiting at the Dewar farm in Saskatchewan, he saw his two sisters galloping down the pasture, standing with their feet on two horses. He said to them, "Do you know that ladies in the United States make money doing that?"

That was exciting news to Claire and Lois, who decided they would do the same in Canada. They found pictures of American trick riders doing stunts. They practised and practised, while Grandma Dewar helped them, telling them to stand straight and tall or suggesting how they could make their tricks look even better. She also made them fancy outfits to wear. Soon they were doing all kinds of amazing feats on galloping horses at rodeos all over Western Canada. And that is how they became Canada's first female trick riders.

My mom herself was an excellent rider and loved horses. Not all the Dewars were cowboys, though. Aunt Julene did not want to spend her life in the saddle! She didn't like the farm at all and when she finished high school, she took the very first train to Calgary. There, she went to Bible School, married and had a family.

Calgary was where our family spent our furloughs. Mom and Daddy went to speak in churches and Bible Schools, and everywhere they went they showed slides of Ethiopia and the work they did. Family and church friends in Canada had

45

faithfully sent money to the mission for them while they were in Ethiopia and they looked forward to visiting these special supporters, so they could thank them and show them that many in Ethiopia had now come to know Jesus because of their giving.

My parents rented a small house at 915 – 10th Avenue S.W. in Calgary, with a railroad track running down the alley right behind the house. Murray and Brian liked to put pennies on the track when a train was approaching, to see how flat the train would squash them. There was no fridge in their house but they did have an icebox. Every couple of days, a horse-drawn carriage carrying huge blocks of ice delivered one to their house.

Murray and Brian started going to Connaught School, an old stone building a couple of blocks away from the house. It was January and almost the middle of Canada's school year. Murray had just finished grade one at Bingham in November, so he joined the Grade Two class while Brian was placed into Grade One. They had to work hard to catch up to the others in their grades but for Brian there seemed to be an extra difficulty.

One day, Brian's teacher asked to see my parents. "I think your son has a hearing problem because he doesn't respond when I talk to him and seems to have trouble hearing what I say."

Mom and Daddy were startled. "Our Brian – deaf? How could we not have noticed?" They took Brian to the doctor but he could find nothing wrong with his ears. So what could it possibly be?

Then it dawned on them and they laughed with relief. Mom said to his teacher, "Brian has spoken Amharic so much, he speaks it much better than English. Everything is so new and

46

strange here, he's just having a little difficulty fitting in and understanding you." She was right. Brian's English improved and before long he was speaking and responding as well as the rest of his class.

It was not long before it was time for the new baby to be born. Mom went to Grace Maternity Hospital in Calgary, and on February 1st, 1951 – you guessed it! I was born. My parents named me Shirley Julene, Shirley for one of Mom's favourite cousins, and Julene for her sister and a special aunt. At 6 pounds 12 ounces, I was a new baby sister for Murray, Brian and Carolee. I never was called Shirley. Mom just thought that Shirley Julene sounded better than Julene Shirley. So I have always been called Julene. I was created in Kaffa, Ethiopia but born in Calgary, Canada and I am happy about that.

Hodges Prayer Card, 1951

Murray and Brian both passed their grades at the end of the school year in June 1951. They enjoyed being free in the summer to travel with Mom and Daddy to the different churches and to visit relatives. In September, they looked forward to being back together with all their friends in the next grade at Connaught School but they were only able to be there for two months. In November, it was time for our family to go back to Ethiopia.

Furlough had passed almost too quickly. In the fall, Mom busily shopped around town with her mom and sisters, buying clothes for all of us kids and supplies to last the next five years. Family and friends gave us lots of gifts, and our church, Bethel Baptist, was especially generous. They held a big "shower" for us and people came with every sort of gift we might need – towels, pots and pans, clothes, shampoo, bug spray, and more. Being the first of Bethel's growing number of missionaries, we felt they treated us like royalty. How we loved and appreciated them!

Also, all during our "terms" in Ethiopia, Mom and Daddy's families sent clothes and gifts and wrote us letters. To receive a letter and especially a package was such an exciting occasion!

This time, Mom and Daddy packed our things in metal barrels and trunks, so thieves couldn't break into them. When it was time to leave, they said goodbye to all our family and friends in Calgary, including our supporters at Bethel Baptist Church. They then travelled to Saskatchewan to say goodbye to the Dewars in Hoosier and the Hodges in Wiseton. This was very hard, knowing that they wouldn't see their families for five more years but it was also exciting to be going back to Ethiopia, because it now felt like home.

We travelled across Canada to take a ship, the SS Roepat, back to Africa. I was just ten months old. On the ship with us was a young family from the Baptist Mission – Maynard and

Thelma Johnson and their two-year-old, Timothy. After crossing the Atlantic Ocean and the Mediterranean Sea, we arrived to spend a few days in Beirut, Lebanon. Mom and Daddy found Beirut to be a beautiful city, as it had been described in Bible days.

SS Roepat

From Beirut, we sailed down to Aden, the capital of Yemen, at the south end of the Red Sea. On the way, the ship docked at Port Safaga on the Red Sea, so everyone could go swimming in the sea. A protective wire barrier had been placed out into the water to keep out the sharks. It was said that the Red Sea had the most sharks of any sea in the world.

We stayed a couple of days in Aden, in our mission's guesthouse. Aden was the hottest place Mom and Daddy had ever been, so they were very glad when it was time to leave. They packed up their suitcases and began to put them and the kids into the taxi to go to the airport to fly to Addis. As they were doing this, one of the Yemenese staff members came running out, holding me, and yelling, "You forgot your baby! You forgot your baby!" They laughed. They hadn't actually forgotten me but had just been letting me sleep until the taxi was ready to go.

The Hodges and Johnsons took an Ethiopian Airlines DC3 plane from Aden to Addis Ababa. It felt wonderful to step out into the cool air of Ethiopia again! Mom and Daddy, Murray, Brian and Carolee looked around at the familiar sights, so excited to be "home." I slept peacefully through it all.

Back in Addis - with the Johnsons

Chapter Six

—∞—

Last Years at Agaro

Mom and Daddy did some Christmas shopping in Addis before making the long trip back to their beloved Agaro. In the shade of tall trees overhead, thousands of coffee bushes were thriving at this time of year. It took three days to travel by truck – an old, rusting machine that seemed to break down every few miles. Murray and Brian rode high atop the bags of coffee and piles of luggage on the back of the truck. How they enjoyed sitting way up in the air, swaying back and forth, or burrowing down into the truck's load and making little hideouts in the spaces between the freight.

The instant the truck stopped, Murray and Brian leapt down and ran to find their Agaro friends. Within minutes, they were racing around and playing as though they had never been away. They had so many stories to tell about Canada – the snow, the school and their family there – and their friends listened, wide-eyed. They would have three wonderful months of holidays before having to go back to school.

The holidays passed quickly. Soon my Mom started getting two suitcases ready for Murray and Brian to take with them to school. Brian was now a schoolboy and would be going back with Murray. He was looking forward to going since Murray had told him of adventures he and his friends had had at the School for Missionaries' Children.

While our family was on furlough, the mission decided to

build a brand new, much bigger school on seven acres of land in Kolfie, a town just outside of Addis Ababa. The land

overlooked the small Kolfie River, with eucalyptus forests all around and vast open areas where the children would be able to play.

Mr. Bill Schmidt was the missionary builder. He built a big, two-storey building, with boys' and girls' dorms on each end, a large kitchen and dining room at the back and a big living room and library, plus apartments for staff at the front. He added a building with three classrooms next to this one.

In front of the building ran a wide driveway, bordered by a stone wall with stone steps that led up to a huge field. Here children could play every kind of ball game. Surrounding the building were hundreds of eucalyptus trees to climb and acres to play in. It was much better than SMC's small land in the middle of Addis Ababa. This new school was named Bingham Academy, after Rowland Bingham, who had started the Sudan Interior Mission in 1893.

Once again Daddy made the trip to Addis, this time with two boys. Mom kissed them goodbye, then went to have a good cry when no one was looking. She had made up her mind not to dwell on the sadness of all these goodbyes but focused on keeping herself busy with us two little girls and the work at Agaro. She told herself she was happy that at least Brian had Murray to help him get used to boarding school. She knew that Brian would not be nearly so homesick when he had his brother to play with.

At Agaro, the Ethiopians kept asking to hold me, another blond little girl with "cat's eyes." By now I was walking. Carolee and I didn't play outside nearly as much as our brothers and we weren't as bold to go find friends and play with them all day, so we didn't learn Amharic nearly as well as they had.

Another Canadian, Mina Moen, now taught in a school Daddy had built on the station and lived in the round house that he had made, along with Mary Thornton, the nurse. We called them "Auntie Mina" and "Auntie Mary." They became very good friends and remained dear friends for life. Auntie Mina learned Amharic so well that years later she became the mission's language teacher, teaching new missionaries to speak Amharic.

Carolee loved spending time at the clinic watching Auntie Mary talk to people, give them medicine or treat their sores and their diseases. Finally, Auntie Mary even gave in and let the four-year-old watch her do an eye operation. The sight of blood didn't seem to bother Carolee, and I wouldn't be at all surprised if Auntie Mary suspected that there was a future nurse sitting quietly on that stool in the corner of the clinic.

Ethiopia has a dry and rainy season every year. In the rainy season, everything grows. Over the next few years, we Hodges children were growing fast too. While Carolee and I lived at home with Mom and Daddy, Murray and Brian were spending most of the year at Bingham.

53

Hodges family at Agaro, 1953

At boarding school, all the kids were required to sit down every week and write letters to their parents. They told of all the things they were learning and activities with their friends. One Mother's Day, Brian made a little card which said, "My mother dear is sweeter far than all the other ladies are." Mom treasured that card all her life and told us about it so often as we grew up that we all knew the rhyme by heart. My parents wrote letters back to the boys, often sending stamps for Murray's ever-growing stamp collection, because he loved to trade stamps with the other boys.

When the teachers sent Murray and Brian's report cards for Mom and Daddy to sign, they remarked that they were pleased with the boys because they worked hard and received good marks in school. Murray wrote, "Miss Wollman says that I am doing better schoolwork than last year. I try to do my best in school all the time. If I can't do it, I ask God to help me."

Murray and Brian took piano lessons from Mrs. Hay on a piano that someone had donated to the school. Almost all the children at Bingham took piano lessons and at the end of the year, the school held a big piano recital.

The Hays and Bingham staff made special occasions for the students all the time, such as baseball games on the huge playing field, outdoor suppers, backwards suppers and camp-outs in the forest. There was also a Boy Scouts group for the boys, and the staff took them on hikes and camp-outs. Several times a year they held birthday parties for all those who had had birthdays the previous months. The children received rare treats such as candies, chocolate or ice cream. Halloween was the most fun, with a large masquerade party and games such as bobbing for apples. Prizes were given to those who had the best costumes and kids spent weeks in advance planning how they would dress up.

Murray and Brian and their friends played in the forest and down by the river. They loved to make dams and catch toads and frogs. Brian once received a jack knife for his birthday and with it he carved a boat out of a piece of wood. His friend, Dennis Ratzliff, came up with the idea of putting a frog on the front of the boat and sailed him back and forth across the water, declaring that the frog was the boat's captain.

Sometimes during the rainy season, the river would flood and when that happened, it was "out of bounds" to the kids. One time, when the water was high, Brian was playing there when he fell in up to his neck. It scared him so badly that the next day, when his friends went down to the river, he went to play on the bag swing in the forest, way uphill from the river!

December 1953 was another long-anticipated Christmastime at Agaro. Murray and Brian finally came home and would be home for three full months! Carolee turned five on December 28th, and I turned three on February 1st, 1954. Soon after, my

Mom discovered she was going to have another baby.

About this time, the mission decided that my parents should move from their much-loved Agaro to a station called Hosanna, a few days' travel away. Mom and Daddy thought it would be best to go when they took the boys back to Bingham in March. So they began packing up all their belongings and the holidays turned into busy days. Even though my parents were looking forward to moving to a new station, Murray and Brian were not. They had so many friends in Agaro, and loved the station. It would always feel like their home because they had lived there for eight years, from the time they were very small. It seemed almost impossible to imagine never living at Agaro again.

In March, Mom and Daddy put all their belongings onto a big truck and headed with their four children to Addis Ababa. They took Murray and Brian to Bingham and said goodbye. They bought some supplies in Addis for their house at the new station and took another truck south to Hosanna, and then one mile farther to the mission station, which was called Bobeecho. Bobeecho is just about my favourite place on earth because it is the beautiful place where I spent almost all of my growing up years.

Hosanna was the capital of Kambatta, a province where people were being saved by the thousands. Kambatta desperately needed someone to teach the many new Christians and help with all the churches that were being established so fast. The mission decided Daddy would be just right for the job.

Our house sat in the middle of the station surrounded by a very big yard. This area did not have lush forests like Agaro because Hosanna's altitude was 7600 feet above sea level and had cooler weather, being up in the highlands, like Addis. But missionaries had planted trees, bushes, fruit vines and flowers in the yards.

Come and have a visit with us, via the little drawing below. This lovely little "map" of our compound was done by Miss Betty Warhanik who is in charge of the elementary school. Now you can see just where we live. I see she didn't get the horse in, but you can mentally put him in his barn which is the little hut just back of our house.

KEY:
A. MACLUCKIE/WARHANIK HOUSE
B. HODGES'
C. DYES'/LAPSLEYS'
D. STINSONS'

E. BIBLE SCHOOL
F. ELEMENTARY "
G. GIRLS' "
H. TEACHERS' HOUSES

I. GIRLS' DORMITORIES
J. BOYS' "
K. BIBLE SCHOOL "
L. BOOKSHOP
M. ATO BEKULLA'S HOUSE

GREETINGS from HOSANNA, ETHIOPIA
SUDAN INTERIOR MISSION

From our front door we could look south and see beautiful mountains, the highest being Mount Shunkola. Fascinating and unusually shaped trees grew here and there. The station had a Bible School, an elementary school, a clinic, a girls' school and dorms for the students spread out over many acres. Three other missionary houses surrounded ours on the same compound, all

57

with very big yards and lots of trees. There was so much room to run and play! Mom often said that one of the Directors in Ethiopia, Mr. Cain, tried to place mission stations in places where there was a beautiful view because he felt it made the missionaries' jobs easier. In Ethiopia, it was not difficult to find a beautiful view.

In our back yard stood a giant fig tree, so big that even when we were older, Carolee and I together could not put our arms fully around the trunk. So although we tried many times, we could not climb the tree but we happily played in its shade. Daddy built a swing for us, hanging it from one of the thick branches.

The four houses on the station were almost exactly the same design. On one side was a large living/dining room at the front of the house, with a kitchen behind it. Daddy soon built a partition in our kitchen so Mom would have a pantry. In it she put a metal cupboard so the rats couldn't get at our food.

Our living room had a homey stone fireplace in the middle of the outside wall, with a small window near the ceiling on either side. Mom used to say that the fireplace was the only solidly built thing in the house. The floor was made of planks of wood, which over the years separated from each other, because the house had no foundation. She joked that at least it made it very easy to clean, as she would just sweep the dirt into the cracks.

Daddy built a long bookcase to form a divider between the living and dining rooms. In the dining room, we sat at a table beside a large window that looked out onto our yard. Beyond it was a small path that led to our huge garden.

On the other side of the house we had two bedrooms with a small bathroom in between. Mom and Daddy's bedroom was at the front of the house, just off the living room. Besides their bed, dresser and closet, Mom had her sewing machine, on which she made most of our clothes.

A door from the dining room led to the kids' bedroom. Daddy built a partition in the room and put the boys' bunk bed on one side of it and the girls' on the other. A dresser and a little closet with a curtain completed the furnishings. On one outside wall of our bedroom, the floor sloped so far down that the boys' bunk bed needed pieces of wood under its legs to prop it up.

In the bathroom stood a table with a washbasin and a tin pitcher, which we kept full of water. We had no indoor plumbing. The toilet was outside, attached to a shed behind the house. If I had to go to the bathroom after dark, I soon learned to hold it in, because I was so afraid hyenas would eat me when I ran across the yard to the toilet. At night, when I was finished washing my face, imagining in my mind that hyenas were just waiting at the door to eat me, I would open the bathroom door, fling the water from the wash basin outside, then slam the door back shut. *There!* I thought, *I hope that got them all wet!*

All mission houses had tin roofs and, in the rainy season, I felt so comforted at the sound of the rain as it pelted down on our roof as I fell asleep. It was one of my favourite sounds.

Murray and Brian, meanwhile, were at Bingham, wondering how we were fitting in to our new home and wishing they didn't have to wait until December to see it. But Murray wrote that they were excited that after the ten-day break in July, Daddy would be bringing Carolee up to Bingham to start grade one. He and Brian were looking forward to seeing their dad and taking care of their little sister, helping her settle in.

July finally came and Daddy and Carolee mounted their

mules to make the long trip to where they could catch a bus to Addis. But that was one of my Mom's hardest days, a day she had never wanted to come, because she would have to let go of her little Sweetie, who was so very young. Years later, remembering it still made her cry, and she wrote this poem:

Carolee

She rode away in the rain that day
On the back of a plodding mule;
She was only five and a half, you see,
But the time had come for school.
And my tears fell down with the rain that day
As she turned to wave good-bye.
She was swallowed up in the mist and the rain
And all I could do was cry,
For I wouldn't see her for many months
And she was still so very small,
And all her winsome, little-girl ways
I wouldn't see them at all.
And somebody else would teach her and help her
To understand wrong from right,
And somebody else would put her to bed,
And maybe kiss her goodnight.
And so it was year after year
She had to go away,
And waiting till vacation time
We counted every day.
So I put her into the hands of One
Who cares far more than a mother,
To watch over her, and to make up to us
All this missing each other.

Carolee was excited about going to school and seeing her big brothers. She was thrilled about being able to ride by herself on a big mule. Years later when they were reminiscing about that day, Daddy said, "You couldn't get comfortable. When you were on top of the mule, you wanted to get down. When you had walked a short way, you asked to get back up. This went on the whole trip!" Part way through the long day, they got off their mules and sat by a pretty little creek, where they had a picnic lunch. Finally, they arrived at a town where they were able to take a bus to Addis.

As Murray and Brian wrote letters every week, Murray would tell how Carolee was doing and he would coax her to write something on his letters. At first she could only write a "C" but he sounded very proud of her. Soon she was writing her whole name.

She found Bingham to be lots of fun. Every day there was something new to see and learn but gradually she began to miss her family in Bobeecho. So after thinking about it for some time, she went up to Mrs. Hay and said very politely, "I've had a very nice time here but now it's time for me to go back home." What a disappointment when she found out that that was not to be! And how glad she was for the comfort of her big brothers. Every day after mealtimes, Carolee would run up to Murray and ask him what the announcements meant. Murray patiently explained them to her because she was afraid of doing something wrong and getting into trouble. After a while, Murray wrote that, even though she was quiet and shy, Carolee began to make friends.

I missed having my sister to play with but one day something wonderful happened. On September 25, 1954, a little boy was born to our family. Daddy sent a messenger to Laymo, a hospital station six miles away where there was an Australian missionary doctor named Dr. Derrington. He came quickly to Bobeecho to help my mom. Everybody was concerned because the baby was six weeks premature. I remember them putting his little crib on a filing cabinet in the living room, and every day adding more and more tree branches all over the room, because leaves give off oxygen, and they hoped this would help his small, under-developed lungs to breathe. They named him Gordon Philip (after Mom's brother, Gordon).

On October 5th, Auntie Avis came over to our house to give me a bath – in the morning! This was highly unusual but I didn't mind for I loved baths; and I loved Auntie Avis. She was always so much fun to be with. She was telling me stories and we were having a good time, when suddenly I looked around and asked, "Where is the baby?"

She took my hands in hers, looked into my eyes and said to me, "He is with Jesus." I was only three and a half but I burst into tears and sobbed as though my heart had broken.

Mom and Daddy had asked Auntie Avis to come give me a bath to distract me while they were having a burial service, committing their tiny boy into the hands of their heavenly Father. The whole community had known about this baby too, so now they all came out to help our family grieve. Another little Hodges baby was buried in Ethiopia, this one in Bobeecho.

For some reason, Daddy did not put a cross on this grave. I always wondered why. Many times over the years I would go stand and look at the little mound out beside our big garden and think of my baby brother, who was now in heaven with Vernon and the twins.

Chapter Seven

Happy Bobeecho Days

With my brothers and sister at Bingham, I was now the only child at home.

It seemed like Mom was always sewing. She had to sew for the whole family. Mom used to enjoy sewing for me, dressing me up, doing my hair, and taking pictures.

She had a Singer sewing machine that ran by rocking a treadle back and forth with her feet. I would stand by her, chattering to her and looking through her button bag, which hung on the wall. I took it down and played with all the fancy buttons, the matching buttons, the big buttons and the pretty, sparkly buttons.

There was a clinic on the station at that time run by a nurse named Roger Nagel. He was a gentle and soft-spoken man and I adored him. Mom often invited him up to our house for meals. He thought Mom was so funny and would laugh at the crazy things she said. One morning she invited him for tea. As they sat at our dining room table, she lifted the teapot high and poured him a cup, and said, "Roger, tea is the fondest thing I'm of." Roger thought that was hilarious.

Mom and Daddy hired a cook whose name was Tesfai. He was one of my favourite people because he could speak English and he told me stories, always laughing such a great big, hearty laugh. Tesfai wanted to become a schoolteacher so he worked for us for a few years to earn enough money to go to college. I would often run into the kitchen and beg him, "Tesfai, tell me the story of Little Red Riding Hood and the Hyena!" He would tell it to me, opening his eyes wide and making scary faces as he talked. I could almost see that hyena hiding in grandmother's bed.

Sometimes I pestered him so much as he worked that he would say to me, "Julee"(which is what the Ethiopians called me) "you arr seemply deesturbing me!"

Once Mom had to go to Laymo, the new hospital station six miles away. She always took Tesfai with her when riding so Daddy hired two mules. Mom rode on one mule; Tesfai and I rode the other one. On the way home, it started to rain hard. Our umbrellas were on the back of the mules and by the time we had dug them out, the torrential rain had completely soaked our clothes.

We clip-clopped slowly on through the downpour. Since I was riding in the same saddle as Tesfai, I began to fidget and complain. Over and over I said, "Tesfai, please move over."

He just threw back his head and laughed because there was not one extra inch of room in the saddle for him to move. Finally, in desperation I hollered, "Tesfai, I told you a million times – move over!" He and Mom both laughed until tears were pouring down their already rain-soaked cheeks. Tesfai never let me forget that day and told me that story many times.

One day Daddy picked a whole bunch of mushrooms and brought them to Mom. He always knew which mushrooms were poisonous and which ones could be eaten. He poured them into Mom's apron and, delighted, she took them to the kitchen to show Tesfai how to make mushroom soup. I watched them prepare the soup, while also eyeing the tempting tarts cooling on the windowsill for dessert. At supper, I took one bite of the mushroom soup and spit it right back out. It tasted so terrible that I didn't want to eat another spoonful. Instead, I played with my spoon and whined and complained as Mom insisted that I eat more. I gagged and cried, "I just can't eat it!"

"Julene," Mom finally ordered, "if you don't finish your soup, you can't have any tarts for dessert."

I did not finish that awful soup and I did not get any tarts that night. And after supper I went into the bathroom and threw up what little soup I had choked down. Since that day, I have never been able to eat mushrooms.

Daddy was eager for the elders of the churches in the province of Kambatta to come visit him, talk to him about their problems or pray with him, so he had what he called an "open door policy." People could come to visit any time. Daddy would drop whatever he was doing to meet with them. I loved to help Mom serve them by bringing in sugar for their tea and serving cookies or bread.

When the elders came for a visit, usually they would visit for an hour or more before they actually said why they were there. Daddy sat patiently and listened and chatted with them. He soon learned that it was not their custom to come right out and say what was on their mind. Gradually, he came to know all the leaders of the many churches all over the province of Kambatta.

Years later, some of the Kambattan elders told Daddy that they tested him for three years. They wanted to see what kind of man he was. They wanted to know if they could trust him. After three years, they were convinced that he and Mom really loved them, so they opened up their hearts to them and trusted them completely.

Mom and Daddy did love these Kambattan Christians. Many of them had suffered so much for the gospel: they had been thrown into prison, their houses had been burned to the ground and they endured other unspeakable cruelty. But they were so excited about their new Christian life that they wanted to tell everyone they met. To them, sharing the gospel was the most important thing in life. We used to say that in Kambatta "the gospel spread like wild fire."

The Kambattan Christians were winning so many to the Lord my parents did not do as much evangelistic work as they had in Agaro. Their work and prayers centered more on helping the young church in Kambatta grow and mature. Mom began to ride out regularly in a circuit among the churches to hold Bible classes with the ladies. She also started a weekly ladies' Bible class in the Bible School on Bobeecho station.

Daddy went to see the people in their homes and would speak in their churches or hold prayer meetings with them. Many of these Christians lived in villages where there were no roads so he would take a mule and ride over the mountains to go to them. Daddy was a big man, even though he was only five feet ten inches tall. Many times as I stood and watched him hoist himself onto the mule, I thought the poor mule just sagged in the middle. But though mules are thin, they are very strong. They are much more sure-footed than horses and they don't slip on the steep and rocky mountain trails, which is why almost everybody rode either a mule or a donkey.

After a few years, Daddy bought a great big, old, Italian motorcycle. It was so long that our whole family could sit on it at once. This motorcycle could go very slowly along the footpaths and it was easier and faster than riding a mule.

One time Murray was riding on this motorcycle with Daddy along a rut in the wiry doofa grass. A cow ran across their path, and the motorcycle hit the cow, sending Murray flying off in one direction and Daddy off in the other. As Daddy hit the ground, he said a loud, "Ooof!" This struck Murray so funny that even though he had hurt himself and wanted to cry, he doubled over on the ground laughing instead. In fact, he laughed whenever he thought about it the rest of the day.

We had some neighbours who lived right next door to the station, Ato Bekulla and his wife Lotwa. ("Ato" – pronounced,

"auto" – means "Mr." in Amharic.) Ato Bekulla worked with Daddy on matters to do with the Kambattan churches; they spent a lot of time together and became close friends.

Mom and I often went to visit Lotwa. We sat in her house

on stools that had three legs, smelling the wonderful coffee aroma as she roasted the beans on a round, flat tin over coals, then ground and boiled them. She and my mom would talk and talk.

Cows stood over at the side of her round thatched-roof house, contentedly chewing their cud. If they weren't grazing, cattle were kept in the houses to protect them from wild animals. Chickens wandered in and out, pecking at things on the floor and clucking. Lotwa roasted grain for us to eat or gave us bootla, a peculiar-tasting cheesy treat.

Sometimes Lotwa came to our house for tea. Once Mom wanted to serve her a Canadian meal. Lotwa ate everything but when Mom brought out Jell-O for dessert, Lotwa pointed at it and shook her head. "I ate all the other things but this – I don't know!" She just could not understand why anyone would ever want to eat something that jiggled back and forth!

After Carolee went to Bingham in September 1954, the months passed slowly until in December she, Murray and Brian finally came home for their long-anticipated three-month holiday. Murray and Brian were eager to see our new station and ran all around it, exploring everything. Murray climbed every tree he could find and he and Brian dug a trench in our back yard where they could play war. They called it their "fox hole" and wouldn't ever let Carolee and me go anywhere near it. They told us it was out of bounds for girls, so we played with our dolls instead. The boys loved climbing our massive fig tree but when they started throwing figs down on us as we played under its leafy branches, we hollered in protest, which of course is what they wanted us to do.

Carolee and I used to dress up in Mom's lacy nightgowns and high heels and play wedding. We would take down the sheer living room curtains to use as veils. Carolee, being older, always got to be the bride. I absolutely refused to be a groom and insisted on dressing up as a bridesmaid instead. Our dolls were our audience. One day we decided to ask Brian to be our preacher. Standing in front of us, as we were dressed in our finery, he raised one hand in the air, bought it down with a blow on his Bible and bellowed, "Do you take this woman to be your wife, and if not, why not?" He had wanted to get a reaction out of us and grinned as we howled our objections. How could he not take this seriously? What a big mistake we had made in asking him to perform the wedding for us.

Murray and Brian were delighted to find that an Ethiopian Airlines plane landed at Hosanna every week. They begged Mom for permission to go see it on "plane day" and raced off up the hill to the grassy airport, about a mile away. There they stood, waiting for it to land. When it taxied up to the windsock and stopped, passengers came down the ramp and people jumped out of the plane and began to unload mail and luggage. Hosanna townspeople picked up their things and hauled them back to town. When it had reloaded, the plane would take off for its next stop, Soddu. Then it would stop at Hosanna again on its way back to Addis.

So Murray and Brian would stay and watch for it to come back. They did this week after week. One day as they were visiting with the pilot, Captain Moon, he asked if they would like to ride to Soddu and back!

"Oh, yes!" they exclaimed, their faces bright with excitement. Would they ever! They ran up the ramp to the plane and the captain led them up to the cockpit.

"Would you like to see Shashogo Swamp?" he asked as they took off.

69

Nodding their heads vigorously, they assured him they would.

He veered a little off course until the wide swamp came into view. Descending lower and lower over the swamp, the plane was soon so low that Murray and Brian could see hippos fleeing in all directions from the plane. Laughing, the pilot climbed back into the air and continued on to Soddu.

Mom didn't know the boys had flown to Soddu but she wasn't the type to worry. Soon the plane came back to Hosanna, carrying two very excited boys, who could hardly wait to race home and tell everyone about their thrilling adventure!

At the end of the holiday, our family began a tradition that continued for a number of years – going to camp at Lake Awassa with other missionary families. For weeks ahead, my mom kept adding to a long list on the wall of things we would need for the trip. Finally, the day arrived and my dad packed the car high with our tent, food, dishes, blankets, swimsuits and towels.

The boys complained that when it was time to get in the car, they barely had enough room in the back seat even with their knees folded up under their chins. Carolee and I squeezed into the front seat between Mom and Daddy. The trip took a whole, long day, with the six of us crammed into the car. As we neared Awassa, every time we went over a hill, we'd ask, "Is this it? Are we there?"

When we arrived at the lake, our dear friends Uncle Albert and Auntie Evelyn Brant were there too. The Brants were from Alberta and had known Mom and Daddy even before they first went to Ethiopia. They were the closest of friends. Their son, Howie, was in Murray's class at Bingham. This was a great excuse to get together, have loads of fun, visit endlessly, swim and play. Different families would join us each year but the Brants and the Hodges always came.

The men built and set up a long table with a long bench on either side for our meals. They nailed a big wooden box to one of the trees to hold our food and keep it away from the animals that prowled around during the night. Some of the guys caught fish for us to eat. Mom plastered us with suntan lotion but we still always got sunburns anyway.

After the holiday at Awassa, we went on up to Addis, dropped off Murray, Brian and Carolee, then headed back to Hosanna. The long term at Bingham was about to begin. In July, Bingham students wrote their final exams to finish their grade. There was a short, ten-day break and they would start their new grade. In 1955, we were able to spend the ten-day break with them but we couldn't every year. When that happened, we would not see them for nine months, which seemed like eternity.

In 1955, a young family from Texas, the Lapsleys, moved to our station. Uncle Tex Lapsley was tall, outgoing and loads of fun. Aunt Betty was quiet and I thought she was beautiful - tall, with a gentle smile and long, softly curled brown hair. They had two little girls, Becky Lynn and Bonnie Lou. During their time at Bobeecho, they had two other girls, Barbara Lee and Beverley. Later, at another station they finally had a boy, Ben, and a fifth girl, Lisa Brooks.

I found it fascinating that the Lapsleys had five girls and a boy, while Dr. and Mrs. Derrington in Laymo had a girl and five boys.

Becky, who was a couple of years younger than I, played day after day with me. I was so happy to have a playmate. Her sister, Bonnie, was soon old enough to play with us too.

On April 1, 1956, my mom gave birth to another little boy. But the baby had his cord wrapped around his neck when he was born and he died a few minutes after birth. Mom and Daddy were crushed with disappointment and for many months afterwards felt an aching emptiness.

We always referred to this baby as "Benny," named after my Grandpa Hodges, whose name was Ben, short for Ebenezer. We buried little Benny beside Gordon, just off the path that went by our garden. This time I was able to attend his burial because I was five years old.

That meant half of the children born in our family are buried in Ethiopia. Because so much of our hearts are in Ethiopia, we always feel that Ethiopia is our country, our home, as much as Canada is.

In July 1956, we were not able to be with Murray, Brian and Carolee during their ten-day break. Mr. and Mrs. Johnson, who had sailed on the same ship with us to Ethiopia in 1951, kindly offered to take them with their family to a town called Ambo. Ambo was known for its hot springs and there was a swimming pool there. Murray, Brian and Carolee had great fun swimming and the pool was always crowded. Carolee didn't know how to swim but as she bounced along the edge of the pool, she excitedly pushed off from the wall, not realizing the water was too deep. She started sinking and panicked, grabbing on to the nearest leg to pull herself up. As she sputtered to the surface, she was embarrassed to find that the leg belonged to a very surprised gentleman that she didn't know.

Later Brian offered to teach her how to float. He explained that she had to stretch out face down in the water, and that when he took his hands away from supporting her, she would stay on top of the water. But Brian always teased his sisters so much that Carolee was sure this was just a trick to get her to sink in the water again so he could laugh at her. But he was very insistent, and she realized she might as well get it over with. Much to her amazement, she did float and suddenly thought that maybe Brian might have some good points after all.

After that break, it was back to school again for Murray, Brian and Carolee where they each had been promoted into the next higher grade. Their classes continued through the summer and fall until December, when they could come home again! But this vacation wasn't as happy as the others had been.

In January 1957, my mom became very, very ill. She began to complain, "Oh, I just feel so sick" and went to bed. Day after day, she had no strength to get up, and Daddy became very concerned.

They didn't know at the time but she had come down with a serious illness called hepatitis. Dr. Derrington was now on furlough in Australia with his family. Mom was so sick that my dad put her in the car and drove a long way to take her to another station that had a big hospital, called Shashamanie. Here she could not only be treated by doctors but could also stay with Auntie Avis, who now worked there. For many weeks, Mom lay gravely sick.

Back at Bobeecho, it seemed so strange around the house not to have my mommy there. Meals were not as good because, even though Mom had made an Amharic cookbook for Tesfai, she was not there to help him cook. Daddy was busy and still had to continue his work on the station and around the province of Kambatta. Once he even had to leave Murray and Brian alone at Bobeecho for a couple of days. He took Carolee and me with him to a station called Duramie. There we played with Laura Jacobson, a friend my age, who had platinum blond hair.

I turned six years old during this time but my mommy wasn't there. I wandered around, longing and aching for her to get better. Murray, Brian and Carolee wrote her letters. She was missing their whole, wonderful holiday and they missed her too. Murray complained that Carolee and I were being pests and always messing up the bedroom.

Finally, she started to get stronger but by then it was time for the three older kids to go back to school, so we all went to see her, then Daddy drove on up to Addis. After dropping the kids off at Bingham, he came back, picked up Mom and me and took us home to Bobeecho. I was so happy to have my mommy home again! She was thin, pale and shaky on her legs but she was home. For days, I followed her around, never wanting her to be out of my sight. I had to make sure she would never leave again.

By this time, we had been in Ethiopia more than five years since our first furlough. As soon as Murray, Brian and Carolee finished their exams in June 1957, we would be going back to Canada again. We all went to Addis and saw Murray graduate from Grade Eight, the highest grade at Bingham at that time.

On the page before is a picture of his class with Howie Brant, Van Schmidt, Murray, Bob Ratzliff and Danny Perkins (whom he called "the class genius").

Once again we boarded a ship and headed for Canada. The trip took several weeks, first up the Red Sea where the weather was hot, then across the beautifully pleasant Mediterranean Sea. After that, we entered the cold waters of the Atlantic Ocean. Finally we docked in Halifax, Nova Scotia on the eastern coast of Canada. We were on our second furlough!

Chapter Eight

The Hardest Good-bye

After our family landed in Halifax, we stayed for a few nights in an old hotel in a scary part of town. One day, Carolee was walking down the hall toward the stairs when two policemen stopped her. "Stay right where you are and don't move!" they commanded.

Carolee shrank into a corner until she saw them coming back, dragging a drunk man between them. She didn't move for several minutes, thinking they might come take her too. Finally, she was brave enough to scamper back to our room.

Daddy bought a 1951 Chevrolet car and we began the long drive across Canada. Our parents wanted to make it fun so we stopped often to swim in the many lakes we passed, shopped at shopping centres and had picnics all along the way. Every night they would look for a motel that had a pool.

There was room for three people in the back of the car and three in the front. Because it was a big old car, it was hard for me to see out from the back seat and I always wanted to sit in the front. Mom told me I had to stay in the back.

"But why?"

"Because you're a wiggle-wog," she answered.

"How come Murray always gets to sit in the front?" I asked.

"Because he sits still."

My shoulders drooped and my face fell into a pout at the hopelessness of my situation. I didn't understand it but I had no choice.

We stopped in Ontario to visit Mom's Uncle Ken Dewar and his wife, Rena. He gave Murray and Brian a whole twenty dollars and told them they had to spend it all before we reached Calgary. To make sure they didn't save any of it, he told them they had to send back to him anything that was left over. They were so excited! Once they were used to the idea, it wasn't hard to find things to spend the money on – comic books, candy, gum, Dinky trucks – so that by the time we reached Calgary, the only thing they sent back to Uncle Ken was a flattened penny they had put on the railroad track.

When we finally reached Saskatchewan, we drove to Wiseton to visit Uncle Ken Hodges' family and dear, sweet Grandma Hodges with her precise British accent. We were delighted to meet our cousins, Judy and Betty and spent a few quiet, contented days playing with them and enjoying getting to know them. From there, we drove on to Hoosier, where a whole bunch of Dewar cousins was waiting for us. What a noisy, happy reunion that was!

Grandpa Dewar had what people called a dry humour. He would say funny things without cracking a smile. When one of his grandkids became too rambunctious he would say, "Give that kid a lickin'." People would chuckle because they knew he was teasing. One time I was acting up and making lots of noise, and everyone heard Grandpa say, "Give that kid a lickin'." They thought he was making a joke again until he muttered softly, "And this time I mean it."

With my brothers and sister at school I had been an "only child" in Bobeecho. On that furlough, I had to share my parents' attention with all my siblings, and I wasn't happy about that. So I was doing all sorts of things to get their attention until everybody started to agree with Grandpa.

We finally went on to Calgary, where we found a home to rent at 432 – 36 Avenue N.W., four blocks from Berean Bible College. That was the same college my parents attended in the early 1940s, only then it was in downtown Calgary and was called "Prophetic Bible Institute." When it moved to a new location, the name was changed to Berean Bible College. That college would play a big part in all our lives in the coming years.

Mr. Bill Anderson came to our house each week to teach us four kids piano lessons. Murray and Brian always jokingly referred to him as "Blanderson." He was the choir director and music teacher at Berean and he was also our neighbour, living in a house across our back alley. I was now in Grade One so he was my first piano teacher.

That year, Murray and Brian went to Balmoral Junior High School. Like Connaught School on our first furlough, it was a big stone building. Another student by the name of Ralph Klein went to Balmoral that same year. Years later, he became a popular mayor of Calgary then was elected the Premier of Alberta.

Carolee and I went to Buchanan School, a few blocks from our house. I did not have any idea what school was like and everything seemed so vast and different. Hundreds of kids went to the school, the classrooms were big and there were teachers everywhere. I remember feeling lost and confused. I didn't know how things were done in this place. My teacher tried to help me, assisting me as I put on my coat and boots and reminding me not to forget my mittens. She knew I had just come from Africa. I settled in as best I could and did well in my studies but I never stopped feeling lost and overwhelmed.

Carolee used to insist on racing home after school. She was so happy to be able to go home every day to our loving family.

What a wonderful change from boarding school where she couldn't see them for months and months.

The first time it snowed, we were so thrilled we stayed outside and played until our hands were so cold we couldn't stand it anymore. Shivering, we ran into the house and straight to the sink where we plunged our hands under warm running water then shrieked and jerked our hands away. It felt like we were being pricked with a hundred pins. Nobody had warned us that you have to warm up your hands slowly, starting with cool water.

I had been looking forward to this furlough for many reasons. I wanted to taste snow. I wanted to lie down in the snow and move my arms back and forth to make "snow angels" that Murray and Brian had told me about. But when the winter months came, the weather grew bitterly cold as Carolee and I walked to school. I had never dreamed of anything like it. I announced to my family that when I went back to Ethiopia, I would tell my friends that in Canada it was so cold, my face stung!

Daddy and Mom were invited to speak in many churches and we almost always travelled with them. As they showed their slides, Daddy told the people about their new assignment in the province of Kambatta, where thousands of people were getting saved all the time. He told about all the persecution these people suffered but how joyfully they kept sharing the gospel. They were so happy to have such changed lives that they wanted everyone else to experience salvation, too. Whenever they were thrown into jail, they would tell everyone in jail about Jesus until most of the other prisoners became believers. When they were beaten, or if people burned down their houses, killed family members or threatened them, they still kept preaching.

Daddy said you could tell which people were Christians, because they were the only ones who smiled. The other people were trapped in witchcraft, desperately poor and unhappy, always having to do many cruel things to try to keep the witchdoctor from cursing them. They lived their lives in great fear of Satan. But the gospel was spreading fast, and Kambatta was changing.

We really enjoyed our church in Calgary, Bethel Baptist. All the people knew who we were and our Sundays with them were special times. They were pleased to hear about our parents' work in the province of Kambatta because it meant that the support they sent to the mission for us was helping so many people come to Jesus. As before, our family sent out a "prayer card" that year, to remind people we met to think of us and pray for our work in Ethiopia.

Pray for Us and our work with the *Ethiopian Churches*

MILDRED and MANLEY
Carolee Brian   HODGES   Julene Murray

Not long after my seventh birthday, Mom discovered she was pregnant. This time she was not pleased. She had lost so many babies that she was certain she would lose this baby, too. She didn't even buy baby clothes to take back to Ethiopia. To make matters worse, while she was pregnant, she was rushed to the hospital for an emergency operation to have her gall bladder removed! But the baby kept on growing and doing well.

The months passed, school finished and we went to spend time with our relatives and friends for the summer. Finally, it was time to drive east in preparation for going back to Ethiopia. This time, all the way across Canada, our entire family had a terrible sinking dread in our stomachs because we knew we would have to say goodbye to Murray and Brian. Since there was no high school for them to attend in Ethiopia, they would be living at Gowans Home in Collingwood, Ontario. This was a place for missionaries' older children to live while they attended local schools. It was named after Walter Gowans, one of the three men that had helped start the Sudan Interior Mission in 1893. We would be leaving Murray, now 15, and Brian, almost 14, for five whole years without seeing them. It was too painful to imagine.

Gowans Home proved to be a beautiful mansion with wide, polished, wooden staircases and stately rooms with high ceilings. Outside, a large yard held huge trees, swaying and shading the thick, green lawn. We toured the home and saw where the boys' rooms would be. We met some of the other kids and talked to the staff, all the while trying to prepare ourselves to say the hardest goodbye of our lives.

Finally, the moment came. The boys couldn't smile. Murray and Daddy looked determined not to cry but Brian could not hold back his tears. Suddenly, all the crying we had held back during our whole trip across Canada burst out. Mom, Carolee and I sobbed, our shoulders shaking, as tears poured down our faces. We clung to those boys. If only we never had to let them go.

Mom and Daddy would never stop praying for them but they had to entrust their precious kids to the Lord. He had called our family to the mission field and we had always known it would be a life of sacrifices. Kambattan believers suffered much for the gospel. We could expect no less, even though our suffering was different.

We finally kissed them each a last good-bye, drove away, waving until they were out of sight. We headed on to Toronto, where the mission had its Canadian headquarters, gloomily looking out the windows and crying much of the way. The next few days we tried to keep so busy we didn't have time to think.

We drove to New York, where we boarded a ship for England. It was a passenger ship called the *Ampanan*. It had dozens of activities for children and adults. We had parties and lots of treats. One night there was a masquerade party. A young lady, one of the other passengers on the ship, took Carolee and me under her wing. She found us each a costume, put makeup on us and dressed us up for the party. We just loved her and had the most wonderful time.

When we arrived in England, we spent a few days there. We toured the Tower of London, which was made even more scary when the tour guide offered to show us what it would be like to be shut up in one of the prison cells. We also saw the world's biggest clock, Big Ben and the famous Trafalgar Square.

But the highlight of our stop in England was a trip to Wales. Daddy's Uncle Tom and Aunt Eva lived in Cardiff in an enchanting cottage with a beautiful garden all around it, bordered by a stone wall. The paved roads were narrow, with tall hedges on each side. We loved Uncle Tom and Aunt Eva and when we left, they gave us a book of Welsh Fairy Tales, which always reminded us of the delightful time we spent there.

Carolee and Julene with Aunt Eva in Wales

We left England on the *RMS Carthage* and headed for Ethiopia. In a couple of weeks we arrived in Addis Ababa, back among the wonderful, familiar sights, sounds and smells of the land that had become our home. It would never be the same without Murray and Brian but at least we loved being there.

Mom and Daddy drove Carolee and me out to Bingham Academy and went with us to find our dorms. Carolee immediately found an old friend who told her where her dorm was. Daddy carried her suitcase up the grand staircase for her. Mom inquired where my dorm would be and we were shown to a large room on the lower floor. I walked down the hall with her, clinging to her hand. When we got there, we met Mrs. Rashleigh, my new dorm supervisor, who welcomed us with a gentle smile and showed me where I would be sleeping.

Since I was now a Grade Two student, I was assigned to a top bunk. It was higher than any bunk I had ever seen. Mom stayed to help me unpack and put my clothes into the drawer assigned to me. Other girls stood about, glancing shyly while their mothers and dads helped them unpack. Mrs. Rashleigh walked around and talked to everyone to help us all feel more comfortable.

I had never been to boarding school but for some reason I didn't feel as lost as I had in Canada. I didn't want to see Mom and Daddy go but I knew they were staying in Addis for a few days, so I would see them again on the weekend. When they left, Carolee came downstairs and helped me settle in and answered my many questions.

After that, it seemed to me that my sister always had to be so far away. Her dorm was located in another part of the building. I expected that I would have to ask her for help a lot, just like she had relied on Murray when she was in Grade One but I soon ran into friends I had known before. Laura, my little platinum-blonde friend from Duramie was also in Grade Two. There were others I recognized as well and soon we were playing happily together. I felt more "at home" here than I had at Buchanan School in Canada because I was with friends I had known before. Not only that but we were in Ethiopia, which was home to all of us.

Chapter Nine

—◌—

Beginning Boarding School and
God's Sweet Gift to Mom and Daddy

The light went on in our dorm. It was 6:30 and morning light was starting to come in the long windows at the end of the dorm.

"Time to get up, girls," said Mrs. Rashleigh, our dorm supervisor, in her soft voice, balancing a baby on her hip. "Get dressed quickly because devotions will start in only half an hour. After you dress, I want you each to make your bed neatly," she instructed us. Mrs. Rashleigh was tall and slim, with long brown hair arranged up on her head. I learned much later that when she came to Ethiopia as a single lady, the man who was to become her husband had been praying for a wife with long hair.

I yawned and stretched, then flung my blankets off and headed for the railings to climb down from the top bunk. Our bunks were tall, spaced across the well-waxed wooden floors in a big room with high ceilings. A couple of wardrobe closets by the door and the dressers along the wall were its only other furnishings.

I went into the bathroom, another room with tall ceilings and small windows up high. There were bathroom stalls on one wall, two showers across from them and a closed-in bathtub on the opposite wall. Our toothbrushes hung in rows over the sinks beside the tub, and along another wall, our towels were draped over pegs. Everything was labelled, our toothbrushes, towels, everything.

85

After putting on my dress, sweater, socks and shoes, I fished in my drawer for my comb and ran it through my hair then climbed back up on my bunk to make my bed. Around me, the other girls chattered as they dressed. At 7:00 we were ready, and walked down the hall from our dorm, past the wide staircase with its bannister, which led up to where Carolee's dorm was. From the other end of the building, boys noisily streamed out of their dorms and we all met in the big living room.

It was a wide empty room with furniture around the outside walls. There was a fireplace, on which sat a small glass clock with four golden balls swinging round and round to tick off the time. Around the fireplace were black and white tiles and above it hung a beautiful picture of Jesus, which I always loved.

Connected to this room was the library, which was the same size. The two large rooms shared a lovely, polished wooden floor and were separated by a long wall of accordion doors. These doors were open most of the time, making a room so large it could hold quite a big crowd. Each room had a front door opening onto the big front porch as well as another doorway on the opposite wall that led into a long hall. There was a piano in each room.

At either end of this long double room was a small apartment for staff members. Mr. and Mrs. Rashleigh lived in the apartment off the library, close to the girls' dorm. Mr. and Mrs. Hay were in the one off the living room, near the boys' dorm.

"Grade Ones sit right up here by the piano," instructed Mrs. Hay. "Right behind the Grade Ones, I want the Grade Twos to line up. Boys on this side, girls over here," she said, waving her hand toward the piano, near where the girls would sit. The boys would be over beside the long accordion doors.

The older kids rushed to the couches along the windows, which looked out on the front driveway, each trying to reach them first so they wouldn't have to sit on the floor. After a bit of confusion, we were finally settled. Mrs. Hay told us, "Now, every morning I want you children to come in here and sit in the same places, so we won't have any mix-up."

The Ethiopian cooks and outdoor staff then filed in and sat on chairs which had been placed for them along the opening to the library.

Mr. Hay read us some scripture and gave a little message. At the end, he asked us all to say the Lord's Prayer in Amharic with the Ethiopians. I never did learn it very well because I couldn't catch all the words. I said the first few phrases then just mumbled until the "Amen."

When devotions were finished, teachers stood in the doorway and Mr. Hay had each grade stand up and file out behind a teacher to a different place in the building. The Grade Twos went with Miss MacDonald to a corner in the library, where we again sat on the floor. Miss MacDonald was about four feet ten inches tall, stout, with blond hair and glasses. We knew as soon as we looked at her that she would not put up with any mischief.

"Today we are going to start learning Psalm 1. Now, I don't want any more talking from you." She walked over to where a group of boys sat and firmly tapped one of them on the head with her finger. "I want you to repeat the words after me."

We looked up at her, and she started in slowly, "Blessed is the man that walketh not…"

"Blessed is the man that walketh not…" we repeated.

She said it several times. Around us in different corners we could hear a couple of young grades saying verses after their teachers. The older kids, somewhere else in the building, learned verses on their own with a teacher just supervising. They did not have to repeat after them.

Miss MacDonald told us, "At the end of this week, each of you will come to me and say your verses. You will have to say them perfectly. When you do, I will place a star beside your name on the verse chart on the wall in the hallway between the living and dining rooms.

"At the end of the month, you will say all the verses we have learned this month together, again with no mistakes, and then I will give you a blue star." It did not take long to realize that receiving all those stars was very important at Bingham Academy!

Back in 1957, Murray and Brian had both studied hard for weeks to be able to say five hundred verses all at once, with no mistakes, something Mr. and Mrs. Hay really encouraged students to do. They finally did say them, and were rewarded with an overnight trip to Lake Bishoftu, the mission's beautiful vacation home on a crater lake, an hour's drive from Addis. Also, they were each given a new Bible.

After verse group, we were directed into the dining room for breakfast. The dining room was across the hall from the living room and library. It was filled with long tables that each seated about seven children on either side, on long benches. I was happy to be assigned to sit by Carolee. We were given a spoonful of cod-liver oil and told we would have it each morning at breakfast. I didn't mind too much but many of the students gagged and almost cried at its fishy taste.

Meals were an interesting and frightening experience because we soon found that we had to eat everything on our plates and never knew what we would be served. Often kids complained back in the dorms about the food. Over the coming term, we learned ways to beat the system. If we were served meat with gristle, we held the gristle in our mouths until after the meal, when we could spit it into the toilet. Mrs. Hay once had the cooks make tomato aspic, a tomato-flavoured gel. It turned our stomachs and some of the kids rushed to the bathroom to throw up. After this had happened a few times, Mrs. Hay noticed and said, "I don't think the children like this," and never served it again. I knew for sure, though, that God loved me, for we never once had mushrooms when I was at Bingham. And, to be fair, I do remember eating a lot of great meals.

During that first breakfast, it was Mr. Rashleigh's turn to supervise us in the big dining room. As all the kids laughed and talked, the noise grew louder and louder, our voices rising. Suddenly, Mr. Rashleigh rang a little tin bell. Everyone stopped and looked at him.

"Okay," he said, "no talking for five minutes. I want you to be quiet and eat." We ate on in silence, looking up at the big clock on the wall. Exactly five minutes later, the roar started again.

Mr. Rashleigh was a gentle man. Although he believed in punishing kids who disobeyed, I do not remember ever seeing him lose his temper. One time, when Murray was still at Bingham, the staff was having a meeting after all the kids had gone to bed. Murray had the bright idea of sneaking outside and turning off the generator so all the staff would be in the dark; then he crept back into his bed.

Not long afterwards, the boys snickered as they heard Mr. Rashleigh turning the generator back on. He came into their dorm, holding his pressure lamp high. "Boys, which one of you turned off the generator?" he asked. No one confessed; no one would tell who had done the deed.

So Mr. Rashleigh set his lamp on top of the dresser, went patiently around the dorm and put his hand on each boy's heart. When he came to Murray, Murray's heart was pounding so fast he knew he was the guilty one. Murray admitted it and received the strap. That story was told around Bingham for many years.

After we finished breakfast, Mr. Rashleigh rang the bell again and called out, "Okay, you can all go back to your dorms and do your housework."

"Housework" meant doing different chores which had been assigned to each of us: cleaning, picking up clothes from the Ethiopian ladies who worked in the laundry, sorting clean clothes in the laundry room onto shelves for each dorm, dusting dressers in the dorms or other work.

Carolee said to me, "Mrs. Rashleigh will tell you what your housework is. You have to do it all this term but it won't be too hard because you're new." I went back to my dorm, where Mrs. Rashleigh gave instructions to all us girls, reading our names and housework from a list she had made. My job was to take down the shoes from a little shelf that hung down from the foot of each bunk bed, dust them and put the shoes back. I sat on the floor with my dust rag and scooted along all the bunk beds until I had finished. Around me, girls busily did their jobs, laughing and chatting as they worked.

At 8:30, the school bell rang and we ran over to the classroom building. There we were told in which desk to sit. I looked around at all the students in my class. I would go to school with these friends for many years.

The first class of the day was Bible. We read Bible stories

and learned Bible lessons and would have to write exams just as in all the other subjects. Bingham sure wanted us to know our Bible well!

The first few weeks of Grade Two were hard for me. My teacher kept scolding me because I talked too much. Once I had to stand with my nose in the corner. Another time she made me stay after school and I barely escaped being spanked. I ran to find Carolee and asked her what to do. She warned me, "You cannot talk in class or fool around *at all* or you will get the strap!" I realized that I had better learn how to be quiet and obey. I was terrified of getting into trouble, or getting a spanking, so I made myself settle down and behave. Fortunately, I was successful for soon I was having no trouble with my teacher.

At 10:30, the school bell rang to announce a fifteen-minute recess. We all bounced up from our desks and ran outside and around the main building to the kitchen door. There we lined up for "morning tea time." We were given two calcium pills in our hand and a little snack, such as carrot sticks or peanuts and raisins. I faithfully chewed my calcium pills each day but many did not like them and hid them in the dirt. The reason we had to take calcium was the mission pharmacist thought we did not have enough calcium in our diet at Bingham. So he made hundreds of calcium pills for us each week in the Headquarters pharmacy. Perhaps that is why I always had strong teeth.

At noon we went back to the dining room. After a noisy lunch, we were sent to our dorms for "rest hour." I did not like it at all. I was so bored, having to lie in my bunk and be completely quiet for a whole thirty minutes. We couldn't take a book or toy to bed either but had to just lie there doing nothing. I rarely slept but tossed back and forth, watching the other girls in their beds. Sometimes we made hand signals to each other. On Saturday and Sunday, it was worse, for rest hour was an unbearable hour long but sometimes we were allowed to read.

After rest hour, school continued until 4:00. What a long day! But when our teacher dismissed us, we burst out of the classroom and ran outside to play until suppertime.

That was when the fun really began. Bingham had a big eucalyptus forest surrounding the entire school. It now had a tall, chain-link fence all the way around it, unlike when Murray and Brian were there, and we were never allowed outside the fence without a staff member. That afternoon, I swung high on the swings, dangled on the monkey bars and rode the teeter totters with my new friends, while boys played baseball on the big field. Some girls played together with their dolls in our dorm.

Most of the students took piano lessons. That first week we were each assigned a half hour time slot to practise and a piano to practise on. When we finished, we were to run and find the next person who was scheduled to practise on that piano. We had lessons once a week. My teacher that year was Mrs. Braden, who came out to Bingham to teach beginner piano lessons. Mrs. Hay taught the older kids. There were now three pianos at Bingham, one in the living room, one in the library and one in the Gospel Chapel down by the road.

After supper, we dressed in our pajamas and housecoats then were led back to the living room for story hour, sitting on the floor again with our classmates. One of the staff read us a couple of chapters from a storybook, to be continued on the following night. I loved the story but it always seemed to stop in an interesting place and I sure didn't want to go to bed at

7:30. I wanted the story to go on and on.

One night, soon after I came to Bingham, Mrs. Cole, the school nurse, was in charge of story hour. Instead of reading us a story, she told us the story of salvation. She said that we needed to be saved in order to go to heaven when we died because, if we didn't, we would go to hell. I was horrified! For the first time, I realized I had probably never asked Jesus into my heart, even though I had gone to church all my life. And I did *not* want to go to hell!

So that night, after I went to bed, I asked Jesus to come into my heart. The next night, just before I went to sleep, a thought came to me, *You didn't get saved last night because you were sleeping when you asked Jesus into your heart and that didn't count.* So I asked Him into my heart again. Two more nights I had the same thought and asked Jesus into my heart again. Finally, on the fourth night, I said, almost out loud, "I *must* have been awake one of those nights, so I am saved!" The thought never troubled me again.

My life did change after that. From that day on, I was eager to please God. I prayed, I learned to read my Bible and thought about God all the time. I didn't want to do wrong. I remembered that in Canada, I used to sneak into the kitchen and steal dried apricots when Mom wasn't looking. Now I couldn't do that kind of thing. Something had changed inside me, and even though I was only seven, I would never be the same. I was always so happy I made that decision.

Mrs. Rashleigh was in charge of two large dorms full of younger girls, plus she had small children herself, so she was a busy lady. We were not allowed to talk after lights were turned out at night. One night she caught me whispering to the girl in the next bunk and called me into her apartment. She talked with me about how I had disobeyed, then prayed with me. Finally, she took out a strap, made me hold out my hand and gave me a spanking. I went back to my bunk and burst into tears. I was scared and longed to be home again. How could I ever remember and keep all the rules in boarding school when there were so many?

In October, Mom and Daddy came back to Addis from Bobeecho because it was time for our new baby to be born. This time my Mom would be in the big Princess Tsehai Hospital with lots of nurses, lots of doctors and lots of equipment. On October 23rd, 1958, Brian's fourteenth birthday, precious little Sharilyn Joy was born.

Within a few days, Sharilyn turned a very dark yellow. She had a bad case of jaundice. The doctor took a sample of Mom's and Daddy's blood and found out that my mom's blood was RH negative and my dad's was RH positive, which is very dangerous for babies. Mom had been pregnant all those times and did not find this out until Sharilyn, her tenth child, was born.

Fortunately, it proved not to be a big problem. The doctors treated Sharilyn and soon she and Mom were able to leave the hospital and go back to Headquarters. Carolee and I were allowed to leave Bingham on the weekend and be with our new little sister. How tiny she was! We took turns holding her carefully and could only dream of how exciting it would be to have a baby sister to play with during our holidays at home in Bobeecho.

Sharilyn turned out to be a very special gift to our family from God. Mom and Daddy had had to leave their two oldest children in Canada for five years, they had to leave Carolee and me at Bingham for many months at a time but God gave them a little girl at home to ease their loneliness. Sharilyn was a calm, happy and contented child, so good. Just like her middle name, Joy, she brought them great joy and they were always so thankful to the Lord for having given them such a sweet gift.

Mom and sweet Sharilyn Joy, 1958, Bobeecho

Chapter Ten

—∞—

The Happiest Days of All

The first term at Bingham passed quite quickly and December came before we knew it. Carolee and I excitedly packed all our things, barely able to wait for school to be over, when Daddy would drive up to Addis to get us. Finally, one bright, sunny, dry-season day in early December, classes ended and the school driveway began filling up with cars. Kids were dashing here and there, shouting with excitement; parents stood around laughing and visiting, happy to be able to see old friends again.

Carolee and I stood impatiently on the porch, looking for Daddy's Land Rover to come up from the gate to the main building. Finally, we saw it and bounced up and down as he drove to where we were standing. Daddy got out of the car, and we raced over to him. He bent over, giving us big hugs as we squealed in delight. Handing him our suitcases, we both squeezed into the front seat, bickering over who was allowed to sit there first.

In just a few minutes, we set off down the road, leaning out the windows, hollering and waving goodbye to our friends. Daddy laughed and began asking us questions. We never stopped talking for miles and miles. I kept leaning over the back of his seat to put my arms around his neck and kiss his cheek, hardly believing that we were actually with him. I hoped that I could make these moments last forever.

After driving through Addis, we headed south, down a long, paved but pot-holed road through the dry and dusty Arsi Desert, with its sparse forests of acacia trees on either side. Huge anthills rose in unusual shapes among the trees, some of them taller than Daddy. From time to time we glimpsed a lake to the east, as a number of them dotted this landscape in the Great Rift Valley. Small and slender ladies, dressed in long animal skins, with many strings of tiny beads around their necks and their hair pulled tightly into numerous little braids, herded lean and bony cattle down the road. Otherwise, there was little sign of life.

Late in the afternoon, we pulled into a large mission station, Shashamanie, which had a hospital and leprosarium. Driving down the centre dirt road bordered with trees, we admired this oasis of green in the midst of the desert. We drove past the typical mission houses (the same style as ours in Bobeecho) on either side of the road until we found the one where we would stay the night – with Dr. Thompson and his wife, who were dear friends from Alberta. We went inside where supper was waiting for us. Carolee and I didn't stay up too long, being tired and having a big day of travel ahead of us, so we were quickly shown to our camp cot, where we would both sleep, our heads at either end, and our feet in the middle. Of all things, Carolee was very fussy about not letting our feet touch! I was nervous that the narrow cot might tip over in the middle of the night, throwing both of us onto the floor. We ended up sleeping soundly all night.

Daddy stayed up quite late, talking with the Thompsons about the work in the province of Kambatta, while the Thompsons told about life and ministry in Shashamanie. They both shared news from back home in Alberta. Daddy loved visiting like this and always enjoyed ending by praying together before going to bed.

The next morning after breakfast, we said goodbye and stopped in Shashamanie town for gas. Daddy rechecked his jerry tins on the front of the car, to make sure they were filled with gas and that their lids were screwed tightly shut.

Then we were off, headed for home. We took the road northwest to Duramie, a beautiful town set in a valley between two high mountains.

Between Duramie and Hosanna was the worst possible road. The big Italian *trente quatros* had left deep ruts in the road by driving through when it was muddy. Now that it was December and the dry season, at least the roads were not muddy but the ruts and potholes were dreadful. We lurched along slowly, in and out of deep holes, dodging others. Our car carefully wound its way down one steep hill after another and crawled up the other sides. Usually there was a river to cross at

the bottom. Sometimes there was a bridge, and it if looked safe we would cross on the bridge. If there were big holes in the bridge, Daddy would have to decide if he could fix it or if the car had to ford the river.

Once in a while we had had to drive during the rainy season and our car slipped and slid all over the road. Often it became hopelessly stuck. I thought back to those rainy-season trips as we arrived at the Shoopa Valley, the most dangerous hill of the journey. I remembered the times we had gotten stuck there. Daddy would patiently climb out of the car and look over the situation, wondering what to do next. If Mom were with us, she would get out and take pictures. Within minutes, Ethiopian men and boys would gather from all around. The sound of a car was so rare in those parts that everybody would drop what they were doing to come watch us go by. If the car was stuck, that was even more exciting, as they would think it great fun to help push us out of the muck. I felt sorry for them, though, because as the wheels of our Land Rover spun round and round, they would get plastered with mud. They just laughed and helped us on our way.

Sometimes we would travel a few more feet and then they would have to push us out of another hole. Meanwhile, Carolee and I took out our dolls and played at the side of the road – far away from the flying mud!

I absolutely loved these drives when we were together as a family. It was a delight to see the countryside, the animals and the birds. I waved to people who were walking or riding their mules along the road. I loved catching glimpses of bougainvillea or poinsettia bushes and sometimes my favourite scent, of jasmine flowers, drifted in through the window. I daydreamed, enjoying the scenery and thinking how exciting my life was compared to when I lived in Canada.

We were so happy to have a Land Rover now. Uncle Gordon and Aunt Inez had sent us money for a car. It was the best, most practical gift anyone could have given us. Now we wouldn't have to ride mules as often or wait for trucks to come to Hosanna. Daddy could come and go when he needed.

We made it over the Shoopa River without any problems and started on the last part of our journey. Our hair was caked and stiff with dust and our clothes were gritty. Our bones ached from so many hours of being jostled back and forth.

After a few hours, we reached Hosanna town. We drove through quickly and started down the hill from the airport to Bobeecho station. My throat tightened with anticipation as we neared the station. The best part of my life was about to happen. Being home!

Finally, we drove up through a long row of trees, past Ato Bekulla's house. As we came into the mission compound and our yard, Mom rushed out of the house with Sharilyn in her arms. Leaping out of the car, we didn't know whether to hug Mom or Sharilyn first and all became tangled in a mass of hugs and kisses.

We spent a happy afternoon visiting; then it was time for

supper. At bedtime, Mom and Daddy tucked us into our bunk beds, kissed us goodnight and blew out the lamps. We drifted off to sleep to the sound of soft classical music playing on the battery-powered record player. Our blissful Christmas holidays at Bobeecho had begun.

Oh, what fun it was to have a baby in the family now! Carolee and I both wanted to hold her all the time. I kept pestering Mom to let me dress her, so she finally relented and said I could but warned me, "Don't let her roll off the bed."

I assured her I wouldn't and as Sharilyn lay on the bed, kicking and gurgling, I closed the door then went over to the dresser to look for the prettiest dress I could find. It took longer than I thought it would though, and wouldn't you know it? Sharilyn fell off the bed.

Horrified, I ran to where she was crying on the floor, and Mom came running into the bedroom. I was so ashamed but she didn't get angry with me; she just made sure Sharilyn was all right. She even let me dress her another time. That time I didn't take my eyes off her so she wouldn't roll off the bed.

I also wanted to dress up a lot myself. I carefully made myself a tiara out of tinfoil and begged my mom to let me wear one of her long nighties. I always longed for a pair of high heels – even an inch high would have been heavenly. One time, I got Mom to take my picture but it bothered her to see me parading around so often and looking at myself in the mirror. She took me aside and said to me, "Julene, it is vain to look in the mirror all the time." I wasn't quite sure what "vain" meant but it didn't sound good. From then on I tried not to look in the mirror very much but I still adored dressing up.

We had almost a whole month before Christmas day. I ran around the station and played from dawn until dusk. We decorated a tiny tree, put it on the filing cabinet in the living room, and became more and more excited as Mom wrapped presents and put them underneath the little tree. When Christmas finally arrived, we could hardly wait to open our stockings and find out what Mom and Daddy had put under the tree for us.

Carolee and I often each found a doll in our gifts. Carolee's would have a red dress and mine a blue dress, our favourite colours. Sometimes Auntie Fiona MacLuckie or one of the other missionaries would give us paper dolls or jacks and we'd play happily for hours with them. That Christmas, someone gave me a book. Because I was only in Grade Two, the book was too hard for me to understand but I was determined to read every word. I read the whole book and didn't understand a thing. To this day, I wonder what that book was about.

After Christmas came New Year's Day and a week later was Ethiopian Christmas. Sometimes we were invited to a neighbour's home for a feast of injera and wut. We loved this special time of feasting and it helped take our minds off the fact that Christmas holidays were almost over. Mom would be busy sewing, packing and getting us ready. The last few nights at home, she'd read to us and let us stay up late. She wanted to make those days special before we had to go back to Bingham for five months.

Finally, it was time to leave again. We all bravely tried not to cry as we gave Mom and Sharilyn many hugs and waved goodbye until we couldn't see them any more. Daddy drove us back down the same bumpy road full of ruts and holes, back to Addis and back to Bingham. He spent a couple of days taking care of business and shopping in Addis for supplies, before making the long return trip to Bobeecho.

Chapter Eleven

—∞—

Bingham Days and Rabies Shots

Near the end of my second grade, the Rashleighs left Bingham to go work "down country." The whole school gathered on the driveway at the front of the big building to say goodbye. Mr. Hay led us in prayer and we sang, "God Be With You 'Til We Meet Again." We waved as they and their young family headed out the gate in their big, old car.

To take the Rashleighs' place, another young couple came to Bingham, the Freemans. Mrs. Freeman was in charge of the younger girls' dorms on one side of the dining room and her husband supervised the younger boys' dorms on the opposite side. They moved into the apartment right off the girls' dorms.

Our dorms were large and had very high ceilings. There was a door joining the two of them and high up on the connecting wall there were two window openings, closed off with a board. Mr. Guth, our mission artist, painted a beautiful scene on each of these boards. We never tired of looking at his artwork during rest hour.

Each dorm had from eight to ten bunk beds, with about forty girls. That was a lot of girls for one person to be in charge of. To top it off, Mrs. Freeman became pregnant with her first child. She looked so neat and smart in maternity clothes that it made me look forward to being a pregnant mom and looking chic, too.

Of all things, she went into labour on January 31st, the day before my birthday! All night long, I prayed that her baby would be born on my birthday but little Chrissie arrived on January 31st. Still, I thought she was the cutest and most clever child.

Bingham staff always tried to make a lot of fun times for us kids and we had marshmallow roasts, hikes, outdoor suppers and parties but when Mr. Freeman came, he had so many new ideas on how to liven things up. Best of all, he was a great storyteller. After a party, we would beg him to tell us a story, and our request was always the same: "Tell us a ghost story!"

The lights would be turned out and he would make these scary tales last for ages, keeping all of us spellbound, with chills running up and down our spines. Sometimes, he wouldn't finish a story and we would have to wait until the next weekend for its hair-raising ending. We loved it.

He also organized outings to the Ghion Pool, a big, blue pool surrounded by tall eucalyptus trees, near the king's palace. The king's Colobus monkeys would sometimes swing back and forth, way up overhead in the tall eucalyptus branches with their beautiful, long, black and white tails sweeping behind them.

That is where I learned to swim. Mr. Freeman made a chart with drawings to help us learn how to swim in three steps. The first step was to float with your face down in the water, keeping your arms out straight. Step Two was to keep your head in the water but begin to swing your arms and legs. The third step was to keep moving your arms and legs but take your head out of the water. That was the only swimming lesson I ever had but I was absolutely thrilled to learn how. I could do the "dog paddle" from then on.

The second term of my Grade Two, I was often sick. When we went home for the holidays in June, Mom was shocked how thin and pale I was, so she immediately took me to Laymo. "Dr.

Derrington is the best doctor in the mission at diagnosing what's wrong," she said as we bumped over the road in the Land Rover. "He will know exactly what to do."

After a short check-up, Dr. Derrington announced, "She needs her tonsils out. Why don't you bring her next week? I'm taking out my son Peter's tonsils, too."

The next week Mom drove me back to Laymo hospital and stayed with me during the operation. I was given ether, and drifted off to sleep at the dreadful smell. When I awoke, my throat ached terribly and an Ethiopian helper carried me up to the Derringtons' home. I was put in a room with Peter, who was sound asleep across the room.

I spent a painful week in bed, looking at Peter on the other side of room, who was feeling as miserable as I was. One day, I woke up feeling terribly nauseated. I staggered out of bed to the washroom, where I threw up blood all over the floor. Dr. Derrington rushed me down to the hospital again. He said that my throat was leaking blood from my operation, so he sealed up the wound. After that I quickly regained my strength, went back to Bobeecho and enjoyed the rest of my holidays in good health.

Miss Wollman was my teacher in school for Grades Three and Four. A brand new classroom for Grades One to Four had been built way down the hill from the big playing field. No one could decorate a classroom like Miss Wollman. I think it was because of her that I started wanting to be a teacher. She regularly re-designed her big bulletin board with pictures of Halloween, then Christmas, then Valentine's Day, Easter, spring or summer. I had never seen printing as neat as hers, either. I loved to help her after school, cutting out things for her or doing anything I could.

In Grade Three, I had the most wonderful piano teacher, Miss Slack. I thought the sun rose and set on her and eagerly looked forward to my lessons. She was the friendliest, most encouraging teacher I could imagine, always full of news and happiness. To top it off, she was from Canada and was related to people from my mom's hometown.

That year, she became engaged to a New Zealander, Brian Fargher, and they were married at Headquarters. She asked Daddy to give her away, so he and Mom and Sharilyn came up to Addis. I begged her to come to Bingham and show us her wedding dress. After their wedding, they drove out from Headquarters, so we could all see her and her new husband. You can imagine the excitement it caused. In a picture taken for the occasion, I was standing right beside her, beaming, in a big crowd of Binghamites.

Grade Three stands out in my mind because Uncle Bill and Auntie Helen Schmidt came to Bingham. Uncle Bill had built Bingham's main building in 1951 and was now going to do some more building. Auntie Helen was asked to help with the many girls in Mrs. Freeman's lower dorms, so half of them were moved upstairs into two smaller dorms and she became their dorm mother. I was one of those fortunate girls.

Auntie Helen is cherished in my memory because she loved us. When we girls were lonely or crying, she would come sit by our beds and hold our hands. This started happening too often so she finally said, "Why should I come to you? You come to me." She invited us to come crawl into bed with her and Uncle Bill, in their little apartment across the hall, if ever we were scared or lonely. Sometimes they would wake up to find four or five girls in their bed! That was heavenly to me in a school where I was used to keeping strict rules, especially after "lights out" at night.

Because I always had a great need for affection, Auntie Helen became the object of my affection. I would leave flowers and little love-letters on her bed. I also remember that whenever she announced that the next day would be drawer inspection, I would take everything out of my drawer, turn it upside down to get every speck of dust out then spend the next hour folding and placing things back in to look just perfect. That must be why I still like to keep my drawers that way.

Just before Halloween that year, some of the little kids began complaining of being bitten in the night. The staff members were afraid that there might be some rats or bats in the building that had rabies, a deadly disease. To be on the safe side, the school nurse had to give rabies shots to those who were bitten. One night when I was almost asleep, I felt a sharp pain in my finger and the next morning there was a bite mark on my finger and blood on my pillowcase. I became one of the kids who was led down to the kitchen every night for a rabies shot.

A big table in the kitchen was covered with blankets and a sheet for us to lie on. The nurse gave me a rabies shot in my stomach, which made a huge goose egg appear. When that was done, I was turned over for a penicillin shot in my other end. Auntie Helen held my hand the whole time and took me back upstairs when it was all over. This went on for ten nights. She felt so bad for me as I got more and more huge goose eggs on my stomach that she told me if I wanted, she would leave the dorm light on all night so I wouldn't be afraid. I loved this special treatment and immediately said I'd like that.

After Grade Three, Bingham began to feel more like home, and I no longer felt so scared of getting into trouble. I was learning the rules, finding out what to do and what *not* to do. I

107

firmly believe Auntie Helen's love helped me feel more secure, even though she was only there for a few months before they were asked to go build somewhere else.

Bingham life was very hard for some kids, especially if they were shy or sensitive. I have memories, which still make me ache, of some who found it particularly painful. What I loved most about Bingham was my friends. Because we shared the same dorms, ate together, went to classes together and played together for many years, we became as close as brothers and sisters. We hated to see each other get in trouble or have spankings. I know my life was shaped by the years I spent at Bingham Academy and I will always love those friends, my Binghamites, with all my heart.

However, the whole time we were there, we all knew that the day would come when we would have to say goodbye forever to these brothers and sisters and go "home" to nations all over the world. Since saying goodbye was such a major part of our lives as missionaries' kids, one of the things I most look forward to about heaven is *never, ever* having to say goodbye again!

Chapter Twelve

—∞—

Playing Hymns and Dodging Bullets

On the pavement in front of Bingham's main building, all the students were gathering for the Sunday afternoon meeting, LAC, which stood for "Loyal Ambassadors for Christ." Instead of lining up like we were supposed to, boys darted here and there, playing tag. Girls congregated in little groups talking and giggling. All of us were dressed in our Sunday best.

Suddenly, a loud whistle blew and everyone stopped. Mr. Wallace raised his voice above the racket, "Everyone line up into your groups," he said. "I want the Christian Soldiers over here by the porch with Miss Willey, you Loyalists line up in a straight line beside them...Boys, settle down!" A couple of rowdy tag-players stopped in their tracks, tucked in their shirts, straightened their hair and headed for a line.

"Now, all the Crusaders line up behind Miss Wollman and the Gideons line up beside them, following Miss MacDonald. Younger grades at the front, older ones at the back. Come on, let's make those lines straight."

As people found their correct line, the teachers arranged them in order. The whistle blew again. "As you pass these staff members on the way down, they will hand you your coin for the offering. See that you don't drop it. Okay, everyone march! No talking."

Forward went the lines. Each teacher had assigned an older student to the front of the line to carry the flag, which represented the different groups. The Gideons had an open Bible on theirs, Crusaders a dark shield with a red cross, Christian Soldiers had a flag with the cross in a corner and the Loyalists' flag was a simple black pennant.

Down the driveway we marched, quieter now, past the girls' dorm, over to a path that went by a chain-link fence, down to the Gospel Chapel in the forest. The teachers then directed their groups up the steps into the brown building, to their seats on the wooden pews. The Christian Soldiers were leading the service that week. They seated themselves just facing the stage.

The elected LAC President, one of the older students, called the meeting to order and opened in prayer. Afterwards, he called out, "Now, everyone please stand for the singing of our theme song. Obediently, we stood and sang out,

"I am a stranger here, within a foreign land
My home is far away, upon a golden strand
Ambassadors to be, from realms beyond the sea
I'm here on business for my King."

We sang it every week. I always thought this song meant we were strangers in Ethiopia, far away from Canada. What it really meant was that we are strangers here on this earth, far from our home in heaven, on business for our King Jesus.

Someone gave the announcements and plates were passed for offering. We all put in our little copper, Ethiopian five-cent piece, while the pianist played a short offertory hymn.

For the next hour we sat and listened as the Christian Soldiers led the service. They had practiced all week with a teacher, memorizing lines. The younger kids had just a few lines to say, the older ones much more. One of them gave a flannel graph lesson of a Bible story. Later, two small kids taught the Bible text verse. Miss MacDonald then led her girls' choir up to the platform to sing a special number.

No one was exempt at Bingham from this public speaking. Every year, we were assigned to one of the four groups, which took turns putting on an LAC service week after week. Since we had to speak in front of people so often and for so many years, we lost all nervousness.

In Grade Four, I made a very special friend, Wendy Leighton, who was a year older than I but in the same dorm. Wendy was from Australia but all Bingham kids spoke with the same accent so you couldn't tell. I had been given a game of jacks for Christmas and she agreed to play with me. Our friendship began with playing endless games of jacks on the wooden floor of our dorm after school.

One day Wendy and I discovered some Thornton W. Burgess books in the library. A couple of hundred children's books stood in shelves lining two library walls, with a little covered bench running along the front of them. Above the bookcases hung a picture of Rowland Bingham, the founder of our mission. On the outside wall, looking out to the driveway and big playing field two tall, large windows brought in the light. Wendy and I sat together on the little bench and read stories about Peter Cottontail, Blackie the Crow, Reddy Fox and the other animals in the Green Forest.

We came up with the idea that we should go into the school's forest and make up our own stories. We jumped up and ran outside, across the field where boys were playing baseball, down the hill behind the backstop, and into the forest to look for a place where no one was. There is very little undergrowth among eucalyptus trees but we hunted around among the trees until finally we found a few bushes, which could pass for a "briar patch." There we made up our own

111

game of living in the Green Forest. We invented a secret code so we could write notes to each other about it in school. No one would know our game or make fun of us. We spent hours together reading the Green Forest books and acting them out.

Other days we played on the teeter-totters or monkey bars or swings. It was so much fun having a best friend and our friendship grew as we spent many happy hours together.

That year another friend led me to a discovery that completely changed my life. I had known Joy Anderson ever since we played together as preschoolers and one day she showed a group of us how to play a familiar hymn, "At Calvary."

"It's really easy," she told us, and we all took turns learning it. It was easy but something clicked in me that day. Playing hymns soon became my favourite thing to do. It wasn't hard to find a piano to play on. The large new dining room built across from the girls' dorms had four piano practice rooms at one end. Day after day, I would try to find a piano room that wasn't being used and began to learn one hymn after another.

One day this got me into trouble. A staff member was walking by the piano rooms and noticed that instead of practising my lesson during my assigned time, I was playing hymn after hymn. She told Mrs. Hay, who was my piano teacher that year. Mrs. Hay gave me a stern warning that I was not to use my practice time for hymns. I obeyed for a while but one day she caught me disobeying and as a punishment told me that I could not play one single hymn for the rest of the term.

Oh, how devastated I was! I practised my lesson at my assigned time but playing just my John Thompson music and scales was no longer fun. Many times a day I would dejectedly walk past the piano rooms but not go in because there was no point.

Finally, the last day of school came and I was set free from my punishment. I played hymns all afternoon until it was time to go home with Daddy.

December 1960 is a time that every Bingham student remembers as the "Coup." King Haile Selassie had flown away for a state visit to Brazil. While he was there, several leaders in the army decided to take over the government. Daddy had picked Carolee and me up and taken us to Headquarters, so we could fly to Hosanna the next day for Christmas holidays. Suddenly, rumours began buzzing around that there had been a government take-over and it was extremely dangerous to try to leave the city.

Headquarters was crammed full, not only with parents and their children but also the mission's Council Members who were in town for council meetings. A couple of brave families decided to sneak through the barriers and actually made it out of town but others tried and came back with alarming stories of being stopped, searched and angrily questioned by soldiers who waved their guns at them and ordered them back into the city. The worst thing was that our Headquarters was next door to the police station and, although we were surrounded by high stone walls, we could get caught in the line of gunfire.

The whole city grew tense and everyone wondered what would happen. The next morning, I was walking along the second floor outdoor balcony when suddenly gunfire broke out. Terrified, I froze where I was but soon the shooting began to come thick and fast, so I dashed to the closest door, ran in and ducked down behind a dresser. A young, single man was staying in that room and seemed very embarrassed to have me in there. He tried to coax me to go downstairs but I was not going to budge! Finally, the shooting stopped a bit, so I did rush

113

downstairs into the dining/living room with dozens of others. Chaos reigned at first but soon we were all told to go down into the basement.

Carolee had been in our room on the second floor when the first shots rang out. She ran to the window and opened it, hoping to see the bullets flying by. Disappointed that she couldn't see anything exciting, she made her way downstairs to join the rest of us. We were not pleased when we were sent to the basement. It was a dark, dusty storage room, more like a cellar. Its small dirty windows let in very little light and the mud walls smelled musty. People were huddled in groups among the boxes, barrels and packing crates.

"Why are all these women crying?" Carolee whispered to me scornfully. "This is exciting!"

As the day wore on, however, it was hard to be down in the basement, not able to see what was going on. We could hear the shooting as it got louder and heavier. The mission men discussed what they should do. They finally decided to run upstairs and bring mattresses from all the guest rooms down to the living and dining rooms. Some of these they stacked in front of the windows to stop any stray bullets. Other mattresses went on the big dining/living room floor, for everyone to sleep on. I kept picturing Daddy in my mind, in the heat of so much gunfire, coming down those outdoor stairs, carrying mattress after mattress for us all, holding them in front of himself to deflect any bullets. I was so frightened for him but thought he was the bravest hero in the world. When he finally poked his head through the basement door, we were so happy to see him, we ran up to him and begged him to let us go out of the basement with him. We clung to him as he led us up to the dining room.

That night everyone slept together on the big living/dining

room floor, crying babies and snoring men alike. We went to sleep to the sound of non-stop shooting but when we woke up in the morning it was strangely quiet. The men debated the situation and decided we should drive out to Bingham, which was on the outskirts of town and away from the police station. Only a handful of people would stay to take care of Headquarters.

We all got into our cars, the gates of Headquarters were opened, and we began a long procession out to Bingham. The streets of Addis were absolutely deserted. Gone were the taxis, the cars and the trucks honking their horns as they jostled for space among crowds of people, donkeys, goats and chickens. An eerie silence was over the city. Some courageous people stood and silently watched us from their doors, with their thin, white, embroidered shawls covering their heads and pulled over their mouths.

We were not at all happy about having to go back to Bingham. When we arrived, we found there was some activity to watch from the windows. Several men and boys were making huge American and British flags on the playing field out of painted rocks and material, so that planes flying overhead would not be tempted to bomb us. We had to stay inside all day and turn out absolutely every light at night. We soon tired of trying to make up games to play in the dark building.

But as suddenly as the coup started, it ended. Haile Selassie, not a king to be frightened by a few rebels, returned to Addis, ended the coup and publicly hanged all the people who had tried to overthrow the government. Daddy told us we could now fly to Hosanna, since the airlines were flying again. Oh, happy day!

Mom and the other missionaries knew there had been a

coup because they had heard about it on the BBC radio news but not many details were given and they had no idea if their precious loved ones in Addis were safe, or what had become of them. The days stretched on and all work stopped as they alternately worried and then prayed together.

That day they huddled together around the short wave radio, listening desperately for any news. Mom turned the dial and another station crackled to life as the Ethiopian Airlines radio traffic came on. Suddenly, they heard a pilot say: "Approaching Hosanna airport. My cargo is five barrels of oil, Mr. Hodges and about a dozen kids." There were only six of us kids on the flight that day but his exaggeration could be forgiven in all the excitement.

Mom and the others stared at each other, their mouths open in joyous disbelief. They jumped to their feet, laughing, hugging each other and crying. Together they rushed to the airport.

What a grand homecoming we had that Christmas!

Chapter Thirteen

—∞—

The "Whipping"

When I was in Grade Five, a new teacher came to Bingham. She was white-haired, nearing retirement and was assigned to teach our Grades Five and Six class. I was looking forward to her coming because she had been a teacher at Bobeecho for a short while and I already knew her.

Within a few days, it became obvious she had difficulty keeping order in class. The boys, happy to take advantage of the situation, began to carry on until pandemonium reigned. When she was writing on the board, paper airplanes and spit wads flew across the classroom, and one of the biggest boys would stand up, wave his arms and make faces at her. Hearing the snickering, she would turn around, only to find all the students bent over their desks, pretending to be hard at work.

She did catch two of the most rowdy boys and made them put their desks right up at the front, on either side of her desk. That calmed things down, but only a little. She was becoming more and more exasperated with us and, as a result, quite crabby.

Even though we "Binghamites" weren't close to all the kids in our dorms or classrooms, we felt a strong loyalty to one another. If someone was spanked, instead of thinking, "He deserved that," it became an "us against them" situation with the staff. We sided with each other, felt sorry for each other and became angry with the one giving the spanking. I remember times when students received what seemed like a very severe and unfair punishment. We never questioned what the student had done. Instead, the whole student body's attitude turned fiercely against the staff member.

I wasn't really enjoying all the crazy behaviour in our classroom but I began gossiping about our teacher's crabbiness with everyone else. One day, another girl showed me a discovery she had made. She took a small piece of paper and coloured one whole side black with her pencil then she turned it over and placed another piece of paper under it. When she wrote a word on the top side, the word also showed up on the paper underneath. The scribbled side acted like carbon paper. I thought this was neat, and tried it as I was working at my desk in the back of the classroom. I wrote, "Miss P. is a big dunce" on the top and continued on with my work, carelessly letting the slip of paper rest right side up on my desk.

Soon the teacher came by to check on each of us as we did our studies. When she came to my desk, she spied the note and picked it up. Horrified, she read it again and exclaimed for the whole class to hear. Everyone turned around to look at me. My heart pounded! What had I done? She told me in no uncertain terms that I was to wait in the classroom after school. When the time came, she sent everyone out.

She called me to her desk and scolded me sternly. I couldn't believe I had been so foolish. I was always so afraid of getting into trouble and really tried to keep all the rules. She sent me back to my desk, giving me the assignment of writing, "Julene Hodges is a rude girl" one hundred times and saying she was going to see the principal, because she felt I deserved a "whipping."

I wrote out the sentence one hundred times and she came

back from the principal's office. Calling me to her desk, she reached into her drawer and pulled out a thick ruler. She told me to put out my hand. As I did, she grasped my wrist and hit my hand about ten times. She looked at me and said, "I never thought I would have to give *you* a whipping," and dismissed me.

I ran back to the dorm, where all the girls were longing to know what had happened. They crowded around me and listened, wide-eyed, as I told them everything, sympathizing and agreeing unanimously what a dreadful teacher we had. I told them how she kept calling it a "whipping," which I thought should be done with a whip, not a thick ruler. I was comforted by all their pity but very shaken by the day's events.

Years later, I thought how it must have saddened the teacher to read my terrible note, since we had been good friends and enjoyed each other's company at Bobeecho. That was her last year on the mission field, for she retired shortly thereafter. And that was the last spanking I had at Bingham.

In June, my best friend Wendy went back to Australia with her parents. I never saw her again after that. We wrote a little to each other at first but then lost contact for many years.

I always did have my sister, Carolee, though. She and I were three grades apart, in different dorms and on different schedules, but when I felt troubled or homesick, I would go find her and tell my problems to her. I knew she couldn't do much to change them but she always listened and comforted me in her quiet way. I loved her so much. Yes, Carolee would be my best friend for life, even if all my other friends moved away.

Chapter Fourteen

—∞—

Mule Ride Over Shashogo Swamp

Back in Bobeecho for holidays, we so enjoyed watching our little sister grow up. We wanted to do everything with her: play with her, dress her up, do her hair, put lotion on her hands. Carolee's favourite colour was always red; mine was blue. We noticed that Sharilyn, when she had a choice, often chose things that were green, so we always referred to green as Sharilyn's favourite colour. One day we were discussing favourite colours and saw Sharilyn looking at us wistfully. "I wish my favourite colour was yellow," she said. We hooted with laughter. Then we picked her up and hugged her, declaring that she could have whatever favourite colour she wanted!

One of Sharilyn's baby teeth had become loose and was taking forever to come out. It seemed to be hanging by a thread for days, and we kept asking her if it had fallen out. The night it finally did, Daddy wasn't at home. He was down at the Ethiopian teachers' house, trying to find a short in the electrical wiring which had made their lights go out. So we told Sharilyn that when he came back she should ask him, "Did you find the short?" She could not say it without smiling, and he would immediately notice the missing tooth.

When Daddy came in the door, however, he was laughing so hard, he had to lean up against the frame for support, rubbing tears from his eyes. Finally, he told us what happened. He was up on the roof of the teachers' house fixing the faulty wire with his insulated pliers. Two Ethiopians were up there helping him.

Suddenly, one of them lost his balance and grabbed onto the live wire with his hands. He gave a great shout as a jolt of electricity went through him. He grabbed on to the other man to steady himself, giving him a terrible shock, too. They both hollered at the tops of their lungs until the first man managed to let go of the wire. I don't know how Daddy ever got down off that roof, because he was laughing so hard.

Sharilyn patiently waited as he struggled to finish his story. When he finally did, she came up and tugged at his sleeve. "Did you find the short?" she asked with a big smile. He was still wiping tears from his eyes and didn't notice her missing tooth at all. So she pointed to her mouth and he finally saw the gap in her smile. Still chuckling, he scooped her up into his arms to give her a bear hug.

"Daddy, you have such Ethiopian humour," I grumbled. I didn't understand why he and the Ethiopians found it so funny when someone hurt himself. Although, I sure did love it when he laughed like that.

We used to buy our eggs from the neighbours. Sometimes Mom would buy a chicken so that we could have the wonderful treat of a chicken dinner. The chickens and their eggs were small, however, so Mom ordered some large hens from America. They were Rhode Island Reds and came with a big rooster that we named "Goliath." Mom planned to hatch some chicks and sell them back to the Ethiopians. This way she hoped they would be able to grow bigger chickens and have bigger eggs for themselves.

During the day, the chickens would cluck around our kitchen door, pecking for grain as Goliath strutted back and forth, crowing. At night, Mom locked them into a hen house that Daddy had built so that wild animals wouldn't eat them.

One day, Mom planned a chicken dinner, so Tesfai went out to kill the chicken. Carolee and I ran out to help him catch the poor bird. It raced around the yard, darting this way and that, all the while screeching wildly. When Tesfai eventually caught it, he placed it on the ground and chopped off its head. To our horror, the headless chicken, supposedly dead, immediately flew high into the air, flopping up and down and around and around, its wings flapping. Carolee and I shrieked in terror and fled to the other side of the yard while Tesfai bent over, slapped his knee and howled with laughter at us. From that time on, we would only watch him kill chickens from our bedroom window, inside the house.

After the bird stopped flopping around, Tesfai poured boiling water over it to make it easier to pull the feathers out, which made the most disgusting smell imaginable. When the chicken was finally prepared and placed into the oven, we weren't sure we would have an appetite for it. How happy we were that killing a chicken was Tesfai's job.

Sharilyn had made fast friends with Beverly Lapsley while we were at school. They were the same age and played peacefully together all the time without fighting. Daddy said, "They both have such agreeable personalities. It sure is fun to watch them toddle around together."

Mom had hired a young Ethiopian girl named Tongutay from Hosanna town to look after Sharilyn. Most Kambattans learned Amharic in school as their second or third language but Amharic was Tongutay's first language, so she spoke it without an accent. Mom's plan was that Sharilyn would learn perfect Amharic from her. In fact, the opposite happened. Tongutay began to learn English. She even began to take on our accent. Instead of saying, "Put your shoes on" with rolled r's and

carefully separating each word the way Ethiopians usually did, she would say, "Puch yer shoes on" just like we did. Alas, Sharilyn was doomed to speak only poor Amharic, just like her sisters, while her babysitter learned English.

That same summer, Daddy was sent to the U.S. for the General Council Meeting at the mission's main headquarters in New York. We knew that we would miss him while he was gone. But we were also excited because after the meetings he would be able to travel up to Canada to see Murray and Brian. It had been four long years since he had seen his teenage boys.

Murray had just graduated from high school, finishing Grade Thirteen, which was required in Ontario. He enjoyed his school and had been very involved in sports, particularly football and wrestling, but he was happy that his Gowans Home years were over. Brian, on the other hand, didn't mind having another year there. By now it was summer vacation and they were both overjoyed at being able to spend part of it with their dad.

They remained a few days in Collingwood while Daddy spoke at special meetings in their church; then it was time to leave and drive west across Canada. It didn't take long to cross the country because Murray and Brian helped with the driving. We could just imagine how much they were enjoying being together. They would be visiting with family and our aunts and uncles and grandparents would exclaim how much our brothers had grown. They would get to know our cousins all over again. And, of course, they would go with Daddy as he visited our supporting churches.

Eventually, this time together had to end because Daddy had to go back to Ethiopia. In September, Brian would take the train to Ontario to finish Grade Thirteen, while Murray enrolled in Berean Bible College in Calgary to begin classes in October.

Meanwhile, back at Bobeecho, we were all excited for Daddy to come home. On the day he was scheduled to arrive, we kept running outside over and over again, or sticking our heads out of windows if we heard any noise that vaguely sounded like a car engine. Finally, in the afternoon, Carolee came rushing inside, shouting, "He's here! I hear the car!" We dropped everything and ran outside. Wearing a huge smile, Daddy was hardly able to get out of the car before we piled all over him, hugging and kissing him and talking.

He hadn't forgotten us while he was away. He surprised Mom with a delicate shawl and a watch. He gave Carolee some "Evening in Paris" cologne, because she was a young lady. He brought a watch and pen for me, and a doll for Sharilyn.

That night we were allowed to stay up late, because we were so eager for him to tell us everything about seeing our brothers. He pulled out pictures and gave us letters from our relatives. We talked until long after dark.

During the months of June, July and August, the heavy rains fall in Ethiopia. We hardly noticed the weather when we were young, whether we played outside, or stayed inside when it got too muddy. This year, as our summer holidays neared the end and it was time to return to school, it rained particularly hard. We heard Mom and Daddy questioning whether the Ethiopian Airlines weekly plane could land on Hosanna's grass airport because it was so wet. Daddy didn't want to try to take the Land Rover because of the terrible road between Hosanna and Duramie, where we'd been stuck so many times.

Daddy finally decided to take Carolee and me to school by mule. She and I talked excitedly about this adventure. Mom fried up chicken and made special treats for our lunch the next day, while Daddy went to town to hire a guide and some mules. They came to our house early the next morning. We each had our own mule to ride and put our suitcases on another one.

We hugged Mom and Sharilyn and set off. Amazingly, it

was mostly a sunny day. Hour after hour we rode, stopping for lunch and wondering when we'd ever arrive at the famous Shashogo, a huge swamp over a mile wide and several miles long. We were excited that we might even see some hippos, not considering how dangerous that could be. Undoubtedly, Mom was back home praying for us.

Finally, we saw the swamp in the distance. "How will we cross it, Daddy?"

"It's not too deep. We'll just ride across."

"Really?"

"Yes, we'll be fine. Our guide knows exactly where to go."

We reached the shores of the vast swamp, as it gleamed in the sunlight, and Daddy and the guide tightened up the ropes holding our suitcases to the saddle. Daddy instructed us to take our feet out of the stirrups and press them up snugly against the top of the saddle so they wouldn't get wet. Entering the water until it was up to the mules' bellies, we started across. We kept swatting at the pesky insects that were breeding in the swamp. They bothered the mules too and they'd swish their tails to shoo them away. In the swamp, their tails would go down into the water then slap back up wet and sharp, stinging our legs or backs.

It took a long time to get across. At one point, I challenged Carolee to a race. She prodded her mule to go faster and eventually passed me. As she splashed by, I reached out and grabbed onto her saddle, which was only made of layers of thick fabric. It started to slip down over the mule's belly. She let out a cry as she nearly fell into the water. The mule was alarmed but couldn't go very fast in the water.

She held on to its mane with all her might as the guide rushed up through the water to catch her. He grabbed the saddle and steadied a very relieved Carolee back upright. Daddy hurried up to help him and they tightened the saddle cinch.

"Girls, stop fooling around," he scolded.

That gave us quite a fright, and we settled down until we eventually made it to the other side of the mighty Shashogo. By that time, it was late in the afternoon. We ached in every place it was possible to ache and wondered how long it would take to reach the town where we would spend the night. Finally, the lights of Alabba came into view. We slid off our mules and walked on wobbly legs until we found a little hotel. It had tiny rooms about the size of washroom stalls. Not caring at all, we flopped onto the clean beds and were asleep a moment later.

The next morning we woke up to muscles screaming in pain. Daddy paid the guide and sent him back to Bobeecho with the mules and found a bus going to Addis. We travelled on it all day and pulled into the city when it was getting dark. The excitement and adventure had long since worn off. We were exhausted but still squirmed, too sore to sit still.

When we arrived in Addis, Daddy hailed a taxi and helped the driver put our suitcases in the trunk. The small, beat-up taxi crawled through the streets honking its horn continually, waiting at lights, waiting for slow trucks and cars, waiting for people and waiting for so many animals that I wanted to scream. I couldn't stand the city; I couldn't stand the traffic!

I wanted to be back home in Bobeecho, not going to boarding school. Anger washed all over me. *Life is so peaceful at home,* I thought. *Why do we have to come here?* I heaved a long sigh and dropped my forehead against the window, closing my eyes. What use was it to think this way? I couldn't change anything by being so upset. We would just have to say goodbye to Daddy, go on with life and look forward to our next holiday at Bobeecho.

We finally made our way through town and arrived at Bingham. Giving Daddy a great big hug, we went to our respective dorms and collapsed into our beds.

Carolee and I boasted about our thirteen-hour mule-riding adventure to all our friends. For three days, I could hardly bear to sit at my hard desk because my rear end was so sore. I perched on the edge of my seat, wincing in pain.

We found out later that the plane *had* landed at Hosanna airport after all.

Chapter Fifteen

Miss Willey and Move to Laymo

Miss Willey was my teacher in Grade Six, a lady with a ready laugh and pretty smile. The boys called her "Jeep" after the Willis Jeep which so many missionaries owned. She was good-natured but still maintained order in her classroom. Several of us girls discovered a new interest. After school, we'd ask her if we could write with coloured chalk on the blackboard. We each tried to outdo one another, writing our names with ornate capital letters across the board. Someone would come up with a new idea, and the rest of us would run to the board and try to copy her, developing our own form of calligraphy. Our writing became fancier and fancier as the year wore on. To this day, I love to write words or my name with big, decorative letters.

I still played hymns by the hour whenever I could find a free piano (only not during practice time) and kept experimenting with new ways to make them sound prettier. One day, Miss Willey announced that she wanted the class to learn a new song to sing in our Sunday afternoon service, LAC. She wrote the words on the blackboard and taught it to us by playing it on a record player a few times, getting us to sing along. She turned to me and said, "Julene, do you think you could try to learn this song on the piano to play it with us? I don't have any music for it."

My head shot up and I nodded vigorously at her, assuring

her I would try during my practice time. My practice time was now during school hours. When 9:30 came, I raced over to the piano room and immediately began picking out the song by ear, not caring who heard me. I worked and worked at it until I could play the whole song. Clapping my hands, I bounced up and down on the piano bench. Never had I thought I could play by ear. Only Mom could do that. After going through my other music quickly, I finished my half hour and ran back to tell Miss Willey that I had figured out the song and could play it for the class. She nodded her head and smiled then went back to writing on the board. I realized I was a lot more excited than she was. Now I would try to learn other songs "by ear."

Gradually, after that, I was asked to play for LAC every now and then. Several older girls played better than I did and were asked to do it more often but I loved it when I was able to play. I still had to learn scales, arpeggios and studies as well as the songs in our John Thompson books, which I really liked because they were pretty, but the true love of my life was playing hymns.

That year our family moved to Laymo, the hospital station six miles away from Bobeecho. Mom and Daddy had been asked to go there for a few months because there were only two Australian nurses there, Hazel Brown and Merle Browne. Dr. Derrington and his family had returned to Australia and the mission was looking for another doctor to assign to the station.

Mom was ecstatic. Whereas our house in Bobeecho had been built way back in the 1930s, the houses in Laymo were quite new and had foundations. They were built of cement and in excellent condition. They still had the bedrooms and bathroom on one side, and the living and dining rooms and kitchen on the other side, like other mission houses but the kitchen had a counter, cupboards and a sink. Mom could hardly wait to set up her home. Laymo was still quite central in the province of Kambatta for the elders to come visit Daddy and he could easily ride back to Bobeecho in the car, if need be, or out to their churches by mule or motorcycle.

Moving day came. Our boxes were piled high atop the Land Rover and the inside was filled with suitcases, blankets and kitchen supplies. Just below Laymo station was a river which had a log and mud bridge just a little wider than our car. When we got to the river, Daddy stopped the car and Mom, Carolee, Sharilyn and I crawled out and picked our way carefully across the logs of the bridge. Mom warned us in no uncertain terms about how dangerous that river was. It was very narrow and extremely deep and when it rained, the water roared through in a raging torrent. She said we were never, ever to go down to the river by ourselves.

When we reached the other side, Daddy started across the bridge with the Land Rover. Looking out the side window down at the bridge, he carefully inched his way along, when

suddenly one of the tires slipped down between the logs! Standing on the other side watching, we covered our mouths and screamed. The load on top made the car teeter then tip way over. It stopped just short of falling into the river. Daddy wedged himself out of the car and, holding his body right up against the side, made his way across the bridge to see what could be done.

He tried to jack the tire up somehow, putting a board in to hold it. That didn't work so he decided to unload all of the luggage until the car was empty. He still couldn't get it across so he backed it up to wait until he could fix the bridge. Meanwhile, we had lots of help from Ethiopians who had come to watch us. They helped carry our luggage up to our house and we were soon happily settled in.

Carolee, Sharilyn and I explored all over Laymo station that year. We weren't allowed off the station because, for some reason, in that area hyenas would sometimes wander around in the daytime but we found lots of places to play. I also enjoyed sitting in the strawberry patch behind our house and stuffing as many warm strawberries into my mouth as I dared. In the front yard was a grove of trees whose branches swept right down to the ground. When we crawled in under the branches, we found that the last family who had lived there had cleaned out all the underbrush. It was exciting to find this little hide-away where we could play house or just sit and daydream.

Mom kept barrels filled with water under the eaves, since we didn't have the huge water-storage-tanks the missionaries had outside their kitchens in Bobeecho. She would put alum tablets in the water to make the dirt settle to the bottom of the barrel. She was not too pleased when she caught us girls stirring up the sediment in the bottom of one of the barrels with a stick.

She grabbed it from us and chased us off.

We celebrated New Year's Day, 1963, talking excitedly at breakfast about being able to go on furlough this year. After five long years, the whole family would finally be able to see Murray and Brian again.

That day, Mom said she wanted to take Carolee and me up the mountain just north of the station to visit some ladies. We could hardly wait. We put on our "car coats," as summer coats were called, tied scarves over our hair, and smeared suntan lotion on our faces. We walked out of the station and across a long meadow. Soon we reached the mountain and began our climb. It didn't take too long, and we kept turning around and looking at the view of our station, as it grew smaller and smaller. When we reached the homes at the top of the mountain, people ran out to meet us, grasping our hands and kissing us on both cheeks. They were so surprised to receive missionary visitors way up on their mountain. The ladies immediately began preparing food for us, and we sat on three-legged stools, drinking sweet tea and eating roasted grain. Feeling content, we listened as Mom sat and visited with them for a long time. A few elders came in, wanting to discuss some church matters with her. After talking for a while, she invited them to come visit us any time. Finally, it was time for us to head back home so we got up to leave but they all started protesting at once. "Oh no, you can't go! We have just killed a goat!"

Our mouths dropped open and Carolee and I looked eagerly at Mom. We always loved to eat injera and wut, Ethiopian ethnic food. Mom stood there, overwhelmed and humbled. She knew the afternoon was passing quickly and we had to walk all the way back home but she could never refuse them, so she said we would be honoured to stay.

Carolee turned to me and whispered, "These people are so much poorer than we are and they have killed a goat for us! Can you imagine how much that cost them?"

They prepared a feast and we ate with them, thanking them over and over. When we finished eating we had to hurry on our way before dark, before the hyenas came out.

Carolee and I enjoyed every minute of that very special day and felt so privileged to be able to go with Mom on one of her visitation trips. Like Mom, we felt humbled because of their warmth and generosity. It was a day not to be forgotten.

A couple of months after we returned to Bingham, Mom decided to take a day trip to an area three hours away from Laymo by horse, in order to hold a meeting to teach the church ladies. These ladies would walk as much as four hours to get there and they loved these meetings. Mom loved to teach them. So she set out early on her beloved horse she had named Napoleon ("on account of his bony parts," she would always say).

She took a boy with her, since women were always supposed to ride accompanied by a male. She was very relieved that the boy had been given a horse to ride too, for she didn't like to make a boy on foot keep up to a running horse. They had a very long way to go and needed to go quickly. They climbed a low range of four mountains, sometimes reaching an altitude of 9000 feet then descended again, crossing a river, valleys, grain fields and meadows.

When they arrived, women from all over the province of Kambatta had gathered to hear her teach and greeted her warmly. After many greetings, hugs and kissing of hands and both cheeks, they settled down for the meeting. They sang some of their own songs, beautiful with meaning, of their new life free from devil worship with its bondage and fears.

Then Mom spoke, knowing how very little truth they had been taught in this remote place and trying to pack as much Bible teaching as she could into her brief time. They listened attentively and soaked up her words, while the chickens clucked, dogs barked and donkeys brayed outside. Some of the older women dozed for a much-needed nap. She loved these ladies and knew they loved her, and they all felt bad when the service came to an end.

After the meeting, they fed her thick, black coffee, having given her the rare treat of sugar in her cup from their specially saved supply. There was even a precious bowlful of bread and meat sauce just for her. Their graciousness and kindness deeply touched her.

She wrote the rest of the story in a letter:

"But I had to hurry away for it was late afternoon, and one must be home before dark because the hyenas are on the prowl even before the light has faded, and they will eat anything they can find, even your horse from under you. Darkness falls quickly so close to the equator; it is always dark by 7:00.

"So I set off with my guide again. At the foot of Mt. Abushura I told him he could go home, that I would be fine from there on (I knew the country well). A grown man would have refused, because that was the proper thing to do, so I was glad it was a boy, and he turned with great relief and galloped away, because he needed to get home too.

"And I galloped on. Galloping, trotting, racing through a village, calling greetings to friends that I must get home before dark. Then I got off my horse, reins in hand, to descend steeply into a gorge, crossing a shallow stream, and clambering back

135

out, being almost too exhausted at the top to climb back into the saddle. I trotted on the paths through the wire grass, galloping on the meadows, until finally I went through the last little valley, through the shallow water, up the steep path through the eucalyptus trees, out into the clearing below the hospital to our house. I was home!

"Down in the river gorge I could hear the hyenas howling. It was ten to seven. I had come back in three hours. Actually, my travelling alone was really not supposed to be done but I had no choice since I had to get home. Neither did a proper woman gallop, for that matter."

Oh, how my mom loved those trips, going to teach out among the people. She called it "trekking." Except for this time, she always did take a man with her when she rode her horse. Once she was riding with her cook. As they crossed a stream, he said to her, "Do you know the difference between a horse and a mule?"

Curious, she replied, "No, what?"

He replied, quite seriously, "A horse says, 'How can I serve my master?' and a mule says, 'How can I kill him?'" Mom laughed so hard she almost fell off her horse. Mules were so stubborn, didn't gallop well or do what the rider wanted but she had never heard it described like that before.

Once Mom and Daddy took a thirteen-day mule trip together to visit remote areas of the province of Kambatta and encourage the believers. Mom wrote a long letter to her family about the trip, ending with these words: "Outstanding memories from this trip (aside from the beautiful scenery) are: (a) the hunger of the people for teaching and (b) the kindness of the Christians to us in every way. Altogether we were over thirty hours in the saddle. I'm toughened up now and ready to go again! The treks I have taken stand out in my memory as the most delightful part of missionary work. There is something very rewarding about getting out among the people, and living in their homes awhile, which brings us very close to them."

The mission assigned a lady doctor, Dr. Spalding, to Laymo. The two nurses, along with almost everyone in Kambatta, were thrilled to have a doctor again. One day a man came to the hospital, with his leg seriously injured from a shooting incident. Dr. Spalding examined the leg and realized her only choice was to cut it off. She knew she didn't have the physical strength to perform the operation, so came up and asked Daddy if he would do it for her. Daddy was the type of person that would willingly do any job, regardless of whether he felt he was qualified, if there was no one else to do it.

So the nurse put the injured man into a deep sleep. Dr. Spalding made Daddy scrub up "within an inch of his life," put gloves on him, and he amputated the man's leg. During the operation, he made the mistake of wiping the perspiration off his forehead with the back of his hand. "Oh, no!" cried Dr. Spalding. "You'll have to put on another glove." When the operation was finished, Daddy was relieved to go back to fixing his car and doing jobs around the station. He said that he'd never been scrubbed so clean in his life.

Chapter Sixteen

―ᴁ―

Carolee Graduates from Bingham

May 5th was a national holiday in Ethiopia. It was in celebration of Emperor Haile Selassie's return to Ethiopia in 1941 after the country was liberated from the Italians. Every May 5th, Bingham Academy had "Field Day," with all kinds of track and field competitions. In the weeks and days before Field Day, we raced with each other, practised high jump, long jump, three-legged races and many other events. The year of Carolee's graduation, a girl named Valerie Nunn was the fastest sprinter, running like a gazelle and beating every person she raced.

Just before Field Day, the teachers announced that our girls' age group was far too large and they were splitting it in two. That meant that Valerie would have to run against the older girls and I would run with younger girls. Valerie was, naturally, not too pleased. I had never thought of myself as an athlete but I was the tallest girl in our class and probably the oldest in our whole group. So I had a big advantage.

When Field Day arrived, to my amazement, I won one event after another, accumulating blue ribbons all over my blouse. The only event I didn't win was the overhead ball throw. I aimed and threw with all my might but the ball flew into the front door of the main building, hitting the accordion doors with a loud swish. Everyone laughed and I shrugged, joining with them.

At the end of the day, I was awarded the grand prize for

having won the most ribbons among all the girls that day. Howard Black won the grand prize for the boys. People took pictures of us as we stood holding a small gold cup, our ribbons blowing in the breeze. We were very careful not to look at or touch each other. We didn't want the other kids to tease us about liking each other. It was a brief moment of fame.

Carolee was using all her spare time studying so that she could say a thousand verses. This was something the Hays really urged students to do. So Carolee spent hour after hour re-learning all the verses, the passages and the epistles we Binghamites had memorized since Grade One. Finally, one day she was ready and sat down with Mrs. Hay and recited them all. That evening she wrote in her diary, "Said 1000 verses in 3 hours and 10 minutes." What an accomplishment! She was rewarded with a Schofield Study Bible that had her name engraved on the front. Her name went on a plaque that hung on the wall with the names of the other students who had said five hundred or one thousand verses.

That year my piano teacher, Mrs. Spitler, gave me a beautiful piece, "Meditation in D Flat," for the year-end recital. I had a different teacher every single year that I took piano lessons, and two of those years I had two teachers, making a total of thirteen teachers. When I commented on this once to Mom, she said wistfully, "I wish I'd had thirteen piano teachers instead of only thirteen lessons!"

Recital was on the last day at school – usually in the first week of June. All the students were very excited. Not only was it the last day of school but also all parents who could make the trip would be there. Cars were lined up along both sides of the driveway and in every available spot on the grass. We were dressed in our Sunday best, and many girls even had a new

139

dress for the occasion. Or at least Carolee did. I almost always had to wear one she had grown out of.

I loved playing my piano pieces but I dreaded those nerve-wracking recitals. I squirmed in my seat, nervous and impatient for younger students to finish their pieces. When it was time for me to play, I walked up to the piano feeling like my heart would beat right out of my chest. My hands were cold and clammy. I desperately hoped that my foot wouldn't shake at the pedal again as I played - but every year it did. It was always such a relief when I finished playing my piece. To me, recitals were cruel torture.

After the recital came the ninth grade graduation ceremonies. Carolee was graduating from Bingham that year along with Marilyn Reimer, Janet Waldock and Murray Black.

Carolee's graduating class, 1963

Mom had made her a beautiful, blue taffeta dress. The three girls each wore a lovely corsage. I looked longingly at them and imagined how glamorous I would feel if I were ever able to wear a corsage. Mom had also taken Carolee to the hairdresser earlier in the day and I stared at my sister, thinking how absolutely beautiful she looked – so tall, slim and elegant, with her tiny waist and perfect hairdo.

When the recital and graduation exercises were finished, we said goodbye to everyone. I really loved my friends, and normally would be thinking of how I would miss them but this time I was far too excited at the thought of going home on furlough to feel sad at leaving them. After many hugs and promises to write letters, we jumped into our car to leave Bingham for Headquarters. In a few short days, we would be on our way to see our brothers.

Canada, here we come!

Chapter Seventeen

—∞—

Djibouti and The Ocean Journey

We left Ethiopia on a chilly morning, shivering as we boarded the plane. A couple of hours later we landed in Djibouti on the Red Sea. As we waited in the aisle to disembark, we ducked down to look through the windows, viewing the desert landscape outside. People with light brown skin and straight black hair, wearing white, loose clothing, unloaded baggage from the planes. When the crew opened the door for us to walk down the ramp, a blast of hot air hit us like we had opened an oven door.

We walked over to the terminal and waited in an endless line to go through customs, first outside then inside the terminal. It took a long time to reach the front of the line inside the terminal. My face started to grow red and my hair stuck to the back of my neck. I looked up at a large fan on the ceiling, turning lazily around and around, slowly moving the hot air about and I grumbled about how it was not cooling anyone down at all. I was dreading having to spend four days in this scorching city before being able to board our ship for Canada.

Daddy tried to be upbeat and cheer us up. He told us we would soon be at our hotel and it would have air conditioning. When we arrived at our room, it was cooler than outside but still much hotter than anything we were used to. Daddy fiddled with buttons on the air conditioner but had no success in cooling the room down.

Carolee, Sharilyn and I turned on the shower. We took turns standing under the lukewarm trickle of water but it was no use. As soon as we stepped out of the shower, we dried off almost immediately and were just as warm as before.

The bright spot of that day in Djibouti was going for supper. We laughed and talked as we sat outside on the hotel patio, eating artichokes for the first time and watching ships pass by on the water. As the sun set and a breeze blew from the ocean, we were finally able to enjoy a slight decrease in temperature in this tropical city.

That night it was difficult to sleep. Mom insisted we keep at least a sheet over us. The next day we wandered around the room in our bathing suits. Never one to sit idly around, Daddy suggested we go for a walk. "Maybe we can walk to the dock and see our boat."

"Only mad dogs and Englishmen go for walks in the noonday sun," warned Mom from the bed, her nose in a book. We were so bored we ignored her as we dressed and went with Daddy. Outside, it was 120 degrees Fahrenheit – in the shade. As we walked along, I looked at the people sitting about in that shade, or walking and chatting. Some construction workers were up on scaffolding, pounding nails into a wall. *These people actually live here,* I marvelled. *How does a human being ever endure his whole life in this heat?*

We discovered that the dock was too far to walk to, so we headed back to the hotel. Once there, Daddy contacted the ship line and they told us we could board the ship early. That time could not come soon enough. We packed up our suitcases. While waiting for Mom to finish, Daddy poked at the air conditioner again. He discovered a button he hadn't seen before and when he pushed it, cool air came swooshing into the room.

We all looked at each other, wondering whether to laugh or cry. "Just as we leave," Mom wailed.

Our ocean liner, the *MS Fernpoint*, loomed high above us at the dock and we could hardly wait to board. "This is a freighter," explained Mom. "It is used for carrying cargo but they have enough rooms for six passengers. The mission told us we would have a nice trip."

"How long will it be?" I asked.

"They said two weeks," she replied.

We were excited to be shown to our rooms where we could finally be cool. We could barely contain our disappointment when we found that there was no air conditioning after all. But above our beds were little round air vents like the ones on airplanes, which we could turn and aim at ourselves as we lay on top of our sheets.

There was almost nothing to do. Unlike passenger ships, which have many activities for adults and children, freighters are only for carrying freight. To make things worse, this was a Norwegian ship and none of the crew spoke English.

Carolee and Mom found some books to read, and Sharilyn and I wandered around. Daddy soon rigged up a low swing on the deck for Sharilyn. I knew that one thing I could do was to go exploring and learn my way around all the different decks, halls and stairways.

We said a happy goodbye to Djibouti, declaring that we could now boast we had stayed in the hottest place on the planet. Our ship then headed north up the Red Sea. The Red Sea was just as hot and humid as Djibouti but the ship's breeze made it more comfortable.

That night we put on our nice dresses and made our way to a large, beautiful dining room. We found a wide wooden table covered in an elegant white tablecloth with white china dishes and silverware. Here the Captain, the First Mate and Chief Engineer, dressed in their naval uniforms, greeted us. They welcomed us and said we would be eating our meals with them. They seemed to enjoy having children aboard and included us in their conversation. Carolee raved later about how handsome the Chief Engineer was. However, he could not speak English; only the Captain and First Mate did.

None of the sailors understood English either. On Daddy's many walks about the decks, he tried to strike up conversations with them but had little success. However, he finally came across an old American sailor, browned by the sun and wind. He brought us all to meet him and we enjoyed listening to him speak with his southern drawl.

One night we passed a port and I looked out our porthole at its flickering lights. When I became sleepy, I lay down on my bed and watched the lighthouse beam circling our room over and over until we left it far behind.

It took about three days to reach the Suez Canal. When we were told it was in sight, our ship waited in a long convoy of ships for another convoy to come south. After they had passed through, we began a slow crawl up the canal. Running back and forth on the decks, we exclaimed about all the ocean liners behind and way ahead of us. Sailors scrubbed the deck, working without showing any interest in what was going on. I watched people along the banks and marvelled at the green fronds on the palm trees in such contrast to the shimmering heat of the sand. It took the better part of a day to go through the canal. In the middle, we came to the Bitter Lakes. Here we passed other ships going the opposite direction. The lake was so narrow it looked like they were travelling in the sand.

When we finally reached the end of the canal, Mom came rushing over to us, her face bright. "We're heading into the Mediterranean Sea."

"How long will it take?" we asked.

"About a week. By the way, the Captain said that the trip is three weeks, not two. After leaving the Mediterranean, we will be on the Atlantic for at least another week and a half."

I looked down at the waves splashing against the side of the ship and turned my head to watch the long trail of foam behind us. I knew Mom was happy because the Mediterranean had such pleasant weather but for weeks we saw nothing but water, water, water. It stretched for endless miles in every direction, in a flat line, to the horizon. *The ocean is an awfully lonely place*, I thought, *with absolutely no scenery*. Every now and then we'd see another ship far away and pointed it out excitedly to each other but it soon passed out of sight.

One day we were having lunch at the Captain's table when Sharilyn suddenly stood up on her chair and looked out the windows.

"What are you doing?" asked Mom.

"Oh, I just wanted to see where we were," she replied nonchalantly then sat down, looking surprised when we all burst into laughter.

After almost a week on the Mediterranean, we reached the mighty Rock of Gibraltar, with Mom giving us geography lessons along the way.

We lined up along the rails to watch this huge, famous landmark that we were passing. The Captain came up and asked Carolee how far away she thought it was. She thought the distance looked at least the length of the playing field at Bingham. She reasoned that would probably be much too close, so she guessed 500 yards. He grinned and told her we were five miles away. After that we headed out into the Atlantic. Immediately the winds grew stronger and chillier.

"The Atlantic is cold," I commented, trying to tame my hair flying in the strong wind.

Mom looked out over the waves, lifted her hands and shouted into the wind, "And Murray and Brian and North America are on the other side!"

"Actually, there is a hurricane out there," explained the Captain. Carolee's head whipped around, looking excited; Mom turned around, looking alarmed. "But we're not going into it," he chuckled. "We will bypass it altogether."

The course we would take ran into the Gulf Stream, a warm current that came up from the Gulf of Mexico. So the Atlantic, which I had always thought was cold, turned out to be hot and humid instead.

The days passed slowly until at long last we sailed into New York harbour. "The closest land is still straight down," commented Mom, as she squeezed things into our bags, making sure there was not an inch to spare anywhere. I didn't like that thought at all. I had once dropped a comb overboard and watched as it sank down, way down into the quiet depths below. It scared me whenever I thought of how deep and dangerous the ocean was.

I soon forgot, however, as New York's skyline loomed into view. We stayed glued to the railing on the deck. This time, even the sailors seemed interested. The most exciting part of the day, maybe of the whole trip, was seeing the Statue of Liberty. A big lump formed in my throat as we glided past and I gazed in awe at the historic monument. We were really here.

New York harbour was a huge, bustling place. We dropped

147

anchor and waited until a tugboat chugged over, latched onto the *Fernpoint* and towed us to shore. We docked and bid goodbye to the ship's staff and made our way down the long, metal staircase to – land! I turned to take one last look up at the big ship and waved.

Daddy hailed a cab and we drove through crowded, noisy streets to SIM's main headquarters, a stately, eight-storey building in an older, treed area of New York. To reach our room we went up several floors in an ancient elevator with a folding lattice door that had to be pulled shut and latched before the main doors closed. While we unpacked, Mom slipped out and bought some plums for us and brought them back to the room. I didn't know when I had tasted anything so good. I sat and ate mine slowly, bite by bite, looking at it and trying to figure out if that delightfully sour taste was in the skin, in the meat or right by the stone. I would have to eat many plums to find out for sure.

We loved exploring the elegant building. Carolee discovered a huge library on the main floor, with shelves of books on every wall reaching to the high ceilings.

Daddy decided to treat us to some ice cream. He found an ice cream stand and bought us each a soft ice cream cone. We promptly started eating and exclaiming at its delicious coolness. All except Sharilyn, that is, who stood looking at hers, puzzled.

"What's wrong?" asked Mom.

"I don't have a spoon," she replied.

We laughed and all tried to show her at once how to lick the ice cream then bite the cone. She took her first lick. I could tell by the smile on her face that she thought life in this different place could be quite nice.

Chapter Eighteen

—◆—

With Murray and Brian Again!

We were eager for Daddy to finish his business in New York because the uppermost thought on all our minds was flying to Canada to meet Brian (Murray had already been out west for a year).

After a couple of days, we boarded Trans Canada Airlines for a flight to Toronto. I could hardly sit still. I tapped my foot, jiggled my knees and kept looking out the window to try and hurry the flight. *What will Brian's expression be when he sees us for the first time in five years?* I thought to myself. *Will everyone watching us wonder at our great reunion? No one will know we haven't seen each other for so long.*

I will never forget the moment we stepped out from Customs and first saw Brian. Carolee, Mom and I ran to meet him while Sharilyn and Daddy followed. Soon we were all jumbled together in the biggest hug, laughing and sobbing so hard that we could hardly see. After a lull, Brian looked down and saw Sharilyn, the little sister he had never met, who was born on his birthday. He picked her up and squeezed her tightly and we all started laughing and crying again.

We had a couple of weeks in Toronto at the Canadian mission headquarters, another lovely old building set in a most pleasant neighbourhood, with flower gardens, huge trees and thick, green lawns. Daddy had more business with the mission leaders, so Mom took us shopping. We walked down to a

Woolworth's store. When I stepped in the door, I gasped in awe. Before me, laid out perfectly in bins were sets of ladies' matching underwear in every delicate pastel colour. *Can you imagine ever being able to own such beautiful, matching underwear,* I whispered to myself as I fingered the soft-coloured half-slips. *Surely only the Queen and princesses would wear anything so lovely.* Even when Mom tugged at my arm, I continued to look back and dream. As we walked through the rest of the store, I saw bins of every other imaginable item – clothes, toys, household goods, and jewelry, all neatly displayed and so clean. I knew for sure I was in heaven.

The next morning, Mom took us to a hairdressing school a few blocks away. "It doesn't cost much there," she explained as we walked, "because students do your hair. We all could sure use a haircut and style."

I sat down in a salon chair and a young man came to wash and cut my hair. When he had curled and dried it, he took a comb and did something I had never seen. He backcombed my whole head of hair, and it all stuck straight up in the air. To my horror, he then left me to go find some hairspray. When he came back, I asked nervously, "Can you put it down a little?" He chuckled and nodded his head as he began to style it. I sighed with relief. I had really begun to worry about hairstyles in Canada.

The next week was a blur as we prepared to go west to see Murray. Brian's high school graduation was not until September so he wanted to stay in Collingwood and work for the summer. After attending his high school's graduation exercises, he would come out west to live with us.

Daddy went to a car lot to pick up a brand new 1963 Pontiac to take back to Alberta. Cars were cheaper in Ontario, so our Uncle Buzz Buroker in Calgary ordered one for himself and asked us to drive it west for him. He even sent us Alberta licence plates. What a luxury. What a gorgeous car.

The next day, we were excited to be able to drive the brand new, beautiful car in downtown Toronto. Daddy had his elbow resting on the open window as we crawled through traffic. A man pulled up in a car next to us and yelled at him, "Where in Alberta are you from?"

Daddy looked over at him and hollered back "Calgar–"

BAM! We crashed right into the car in front of us, which had stopped suddenly. We girls screamed. Mom shouted, "Oh, Manley!" Traffic stopped all around us and I wondered what Uncle Buzz would say when we delivered a smashed-up car to him. The police came and took a report. We spent a few extra days getting the car fixed and it looked as good as new.

Soon we were on our way. As on our previous furlough, we stopped regularly to swim, shop and eat. I didn't even mind having to sit in the back seat of the wonderful, new Pontiac, because it was wide and I could easily see out the big windows.

We headed for Wolf Point, Montana, where a huge family reunion was being held for Grandma's Dewar's side of the family, the Taylors. Mom was so looking forward to seeing her Taylor cousins, aunts and uncles and grandmother as well as her parents and brothers and sisters who were coming with their families.

We drove into the campground to a great, big, noisy, and happy welcome. People came running from everywhere to greet us. After meeting dozens of relatives and patiently waiting for a break in the visiting, I tugged at Mom's arm and told her that I really wanted to see my Great Aunt Julene, for whom I had been named. I had never seen her before but Mom always spoke so fondly of her in Ethiopia whenever we looked at pictures of her in our photo album. She looked so serene, sweet and beautiful. Every time I saw her pictures, I was thrilled that I had been named after her.

Great Aunt Julene and her husband, Peter, had been missionaries to Hawaii before it had ever become a state. When Mom was a young girl they came up to Canada to visit the Dewars. Mom was so taken with her sweet Aunt Julene that she decided she wanted to be a missionary when she grew up.

All of this was going through my mind as we went looking for my great aunt. She had already been told of our arrival and that I wanted to see her. I was a little bit nervous until I saw this lovely lady coming toward us with a big smile. She stretched out her arms to me and said, "Oh, this is a very special girl. I am so happy to see you, Julene," and gave me a big hug. I was absolutely enchanted. As she visited with Mom, who was also so happy to see her beloved auntie, I stood there and held her hand, looking up at her. It was a moment I would never forget.

After the reunion, we drove north to Saskatchewan. The closer we came to arriving, the more excited I grew. We would finally see Murray who was waiting for us at our grandparents' farm. As we left the highway for the last stretch of gravel road, I could hardly bear the wait. The car had scarcely come to a stop in the yard before we burst out of its doors for another wild and happy reunion of hugs, tears and kisses. Murray was so taken with Sharilyn that he put her up on his shoulders, sat her on his lap and took her everywhere with him. He laughed at everything she said and soon she had him wrapped around her little finger. How fun it was to have him with us as we drove on to Calgary.

Finally, we arrived at Uncle Buzz and Aunt Julene's place and delivered their new car. They asked us to stay with them in their beautiful new home while they helped us find a house to rent. We found one that was near Berean Bible College, where both Murray and Brian would be attending school. Carolee was enrolled in the brand new James Fowler High School. She was in Grade Ten, the only grade James Fowler had that year. The next year they added Grade Eleven and the following year she was in their very first graduating class. The picture of that Grade Twelve class still hangs on the wall at the school.

I had a four-block walk to Colonel Irvine Junior High School and was soon settled in with a Grade Seven class. It was so different living at home and walking to school every day. When we arrived at school in the morning, we went to our homeroom, where we said the Lord's Prayer as a class and our teacher, Mrs. Barnes, read a Psalm. Whenever she read one I had learned at Bingham, I silently said it with her under my breath.

Our homeroom class stayed together all day but we changed rooms and had different teachers for each subject, so we walked all over the school every day. Everyone was fascinated with the fact that I was from Africa and it didn't take them long to learn that I was different in almost every way.

One of the biggest differences was in music. I had only ever heard classical music on our record player in Ethiopia and all my piano songs were classical. In church, we sang hymns and choruses. One night, a family from church invited us to their home to eat with them. After supper, they turned on their TV and we watched a program called "The Ed Sullivan Show." A group of four young men, with long hair and tight suits came out and sang songs like "She Loves You, Yeah, Yeah, Yeah" and "I Wanna Hold Your Hand." I had never heard a group that played guitars and sang with drums. Girls in the audience screamed, fainted or burst into tears. I could hardly believe my eyes.

The next day in school, all the girls in my class were gathered together, talking about the show. "Did you see the Beatles?" they asked me.

"Yeah," I replied, "weren't they dumb?" Everyone stared at me, mouths open.

"What? Are you crazy? They are fabulous!" they yelled. Oh, no! I had made a big mistake.

"She's from Africa," they groaned, rolling their eyes but forgiving me.

One chilly day, November 22nd, 1963, I was walking back to school after lunch. A young boy I had never seen in my life passed me on the sidewalk and said, "Did you hear that President Kennedy was shot?"

"What!" I gasped.

"Yeah, it's all over the news," he said and walked on.

I ran to the school at top speed. When I arrived, everyone in the halls was buzzing with the news. Not much studying went on for the rest of that day. Teachers stopped their lessons to discuss what had happened to our neighbours to the south. I could hardly wait to go home and read the newspapers. For days we watched Jacqueline Kennedy, who I thought was so elegant, and her small children. We stayed up late to see the news of President Kennedy's funeral on a friend's television. I read everything I could get my hands on about the Kennedy family.

Christmas that year was indescribably happy since our entire family was together. I had never seen so many presents in my entire life. Our church, Bethel Baptist, gave us each gifts. Of course, we also had gifts from friends and family members. We exclaimed over one gift after another as wrapping paper flew in all directions. Brian was handed a thin, flat gift, which was obviously a record. "But I didn't want a basketball," he said with a mock sigh.

Murray, after he had opened all of his gifts, gathered a great pile of them together, balancing them in his arms to take to his room. "Is this all I get?" he joked, as we laughed at our crazy brothers. What a delight it was being altogether.

My heart just burst with pride when our whole family sat in a big, long row at Bethel Baptist Church. Many Sundays, however, my brothers were not at church with us. Murray sang in a quartet from Berean and Brian played the piano for them, and on weekends they travelled to other churches and sang. Often the quartet would come over to our house and practise and we would sit and listen to them, cheering and clapping.

One cold winter day, Mom came into my room and said, "Julene, my mom is coming for a visit. I would like you to clean up your room for her, and you and Sharilyn will sleep downstairs while she is here."

I had so much fun that day, dusting, cleaning and vacuuming my room until it gleamed. Standing back and looking at it, I was completely delighted in what I saw. I opened the window slightly to let in some fresh and frigid air. I ran into the bathroom to fetch an air freshener, which I gently sprayed around the room. Not only was there not a wrinkle in the bedspread nor a speck of dust on the dresser but the room smelled wonderful, too. That day, for the first time, I realized I loved how pretty a neat and tidy room looked. I knew I would want to keep my bedroom like that from then on.

One of my favourite people that furlough was my Aunt Julene. She had such a zest for life and a crazy way of describing things that she was always making me laugh. I loved being around her. We didn't live too far from their family and spent lots of time together. Their sons, Stewart and Jan were my age and they also had two adorable little kids, Tami and Craig.

Aunt Julene suggested we take lessons from her kids' piano teacher. Mr. Benbow was a perfectionist, who trained students to play like concert pianists. He wrote in the fingering for every note and would have students work on one song for months, until they could play it flawlessly. Carolee ended up being the only one in our family to take lessons from Mr. Benbow. Brian's teacher in Collingwood had been a blind concert pianist, so he had never learned to pay attention to fingering. Since Mr. Benbow didn't want to start teaching Brian fingering from scratch, he recommended another teacher for him.

Mr. Benbow asked one of his advanced students, Miss Cook, to teach me. I didn't learn a lot of pieces that year because she was as particular as he was. She would send me home with instructions to practise every bar in the song ten times then play whole sections ten times. She also wrote on the music which finger to play for each note. I learned to play "Für Elise" absolutely perfectly. I faithfully practised as I was told but as soon as I was done, I went back to playing hymns whenever the piano was free. I learned "The Holy City" by heart that year.

One day Murray leaned over me while I was playing hymns. "You should play different chords," he suggested, "like Carol Wickens does." Carol Wickens was Berean's pianist and played for the choir, a trio and other groups. She played both piano and organ marvellously. So I made a great effort to try out different chords. This was something completely new for me but I kept working at it until, over the years, I learned a lot of pretty ones.

156

That year Brian began to date a Berean student, Rose Norton. She had a clear, high and lovely soprano voice. Besides being a soloist in the Berean choir, she was part of a trio that travelled from church to church. Little did I know that one day these two musical ladies, Carol Wickens and Rose Norton, would be my sisters-in-law for the rest of my life.

Murray and Brian went on a tour in the summer with their quartet. When they came back, Mom kept commenting that they sounded even better, blending together in perfect harmony. The quartet members were special guests in our home and felt like part of the family. They eventually recorded a big reel-to-reel tape of all their songs, which Mom and Daddy took back to Ethiopia and played on their great big tape recorder until they almost wore the tape out.

Hodges' Prayer Card, 1964

Chapter Nineteen

—∞—

Flying Back to Ethiopia

Summer drew to a close and it was time to go back to
Ethiopia. We would be leaving Carolee in Canada this time as
well as Murray and Brian. The boys were in college and would
be working and probably starting families of their own soon. It
was hard enough to have to leave them once more but Carolee
was still just in high school. Mom began to experience the same
old agony of leaving her again. Years later, the memory still
brought tears to her eyes and she added some verses to the
poem she had tearfully written when Carolee first went off to
Bingham at the tender age of five and a half. This time they
would be leaving her for five years.

> She stayed behind in Canada then
> When she was just fifteen;
> She was twenty when I saw her again
> And all those years between
> Someone else was mother to her
> Watching her as she grew
> From girlhood into womanhood
> Years that I never knew.
> Never was there to counsel her,
> Or hold her when she cried.
> Oh, God! how many times I wished
> To be there by her side.
> And she had to come to terms with a life

That wasn't normal at all,
But she knew that God would never fail
And would answer to her call.
And always the love of a loving God
Was there to make amends,
With strength to meet each passing day
Because of the grace he sends.

One day a quiet, soft-spoken couple came to visit us. In gentle voices, they said they would like Carolee to come live with them and their family. They pastored a church affiliated with Bethel Baptist, in a new area of Calgary called Mayland Heights. Mom and Daddy were thrilled at what they believed to be God's provision. Carolee looked nervously excited.

Another day not long afterwards, a fun young couple bounded into our home and asked if Brian would like to come live with them. The wife was full of life and laughter and we enjoyed our visit with them so much. I looked over at Carolee and saw sadness come into her eyes. She was reserved and needed to be around people who were more outgoing. I could tell that she wished she could live with them but would never dream of suggesting it. In the years to come, the family who offered to keep her were always very kind but in their quiet home she felt lonely and homesick.

However, every holiday found her on the first Greyhound bus travelling east to Saskatchewan. She spent all her holidays at the Dewar farm with Uncle Gordon and Aunt Inez, whose home was filled with loads of activity, noise and love. Aunt Inez taught her to cook and sew, and Carolee even tried to help Uncle Gordon with baling hay. There were also many books to read and a piano to play. They became her second parents while Mom and Daddy were in Ethiopia.

The day came for us to leave Calgary. Murray and Carolee were coming with us as far as Hoosier but Brian had to stay in Calgary because he had a job. It was so hard to see him standing alone by the garage as we pulled out. When we saw him blinking back the tears, Mom and we three girls burst into sobs. Daddy and Murray did their best to cheer us up but it was a subdued ride to Hoosier.

We spent the next several days driving around to see uncles, aunts and grandparents – both Hodges and Dewar – for one last visit each. All these goodbyes were hard but the last goodbye would prove to be difficult for a different reason.

Carolee was leaning up against a fence. She was dreading having to hug or kiss me goodbye. That year had been hard in many ways. I had turned thirteen and had experienced a lot of emotional changes. Many times during the year I was angry with Mom and Daddy, a brand new feeling for me that I didn't like. I also tormented Carolee terribly, annoying her just for the fun of it and arguing with her all the time. Soon she could hardly stand the sight of me.

When Mom saw Carolee's hesitance, she said, "Well, at least shake hands, girls." So I walked up to the fence where Carolee had her chin resting on her arms. Hardly moving, she stuck out her little finger and I shook her finger with mine. We all laughed. It lightened the moment but in the coming years, I would regret how I had treated my sister. I really came to miss her. When we became adults, she grew to be my dearest friend on earth.

Sharilyn and Daddy took a train to Ontario but Mom and I drove from the farm with Grandma and Grandpa Dewar, who wanted to come to Ontario with us and visit relatives.

I was excited about the trip back to Africa because,

honestly, I had begun to think life in Canada was extremely boring compared to what I was used to in Ethiopia. I felt sorry for all my friends and family who had to stay in Canada and endure the long, freezing winters.

The most thrilling thing was that for the very first time we did not have to go back to Ethiopia by ship. We could *fly* the entire way and be there in just a few days.

First, we flew to Switzerland for five days. There we visited one of the Janz Brothers, one of my parents' favourite quartets. We went to Zurich to sightsee at their World Fair grounds. I saw fascinating inventions, which I have never seen since.

From there we flew to Rome. Mom had been talking enthusiastically about wanting to go to La Caracalla to see an opera. I longed with all my heart to see this legendary outdoor opera house but no, I had to stay in the hotel room and babysit Sharilyn. However, the next morning we went sightseeing to the Coliseum. We walked around Rome, enjoying its fountains and statues, stopping for spumoni ice cream or pasta whenever we wanted.

From Rome we flew to Athens and explored the Parthenon in that bright, blue and white city. Then we caught a plane to Egypt. In Cairo, we went to the Cairo museum, where they had displays about the pharaohs. When we took a tour to the pyramids, I rode a camel – the only time in my life.

Travelling by plane was absolutely wonderful! How I loved that trip. Finally, we boarded a big four-propeller Ethiopian Airlines plane and flew to Addis Ababa. We were back in our beloved home, about to begin a new and very different term.

Chapter Twenty

—∞—

Grade Eight and Queen Elizabeth

Just before we flew to Europe, Daddy received a call from the mission leadership asking if he would step in temporarily as Deputy Director in Ethiopia to replace the one who had gone on furlough. Daddy had no administrative experience but always agreed to do a job if he was needed. So he said yes.

As soon as we arrived in Addis, it was time for Sharilyn and me to go to Bingham. Sharilyn was now a Grade One student. With Daddy and Mom living in Addis temporarily, that meant that she and I could be with them on weekends. However, Bingham said Sharilyn couldn't leave for the first six weeks in order to become used to boarding school life. One weekend Mom told me she really missed Sharilyn then laughed, "Are we ever spoiled! We used to spend months and years without our kids and now I am complaining about six weeks."

I was in Grade Eight. Being one of the "older kids" felt so different. We interacted with the staff more than we ever did when we were young. We got to know them well and had a lot of fun with them. They treated us as though we were responsible and gave us privileges such as going with them into town. Sometimes we went to the swimming pool, other times for injera and wut or ice cream, and still other times just shopping with one of the adults. We were also allowed to go to church at Headquarters each Sunday morning and evening.

Mr. and Mrs. Emmel were the station heads. Mr. Emmel

was a kind and patient man. His wife was loads of fun. She efficiently ran the kitchen, laundry and household. She had an infectious laugh yet could be strict with kids who tried to get away with mischief.

Our dorms were becoming crowded and students were being housed in rooms upstairs that were needed for staff apartments. We desperately needed a new dorm. To my great delight, I found out that Uncle Bill Schmidt had come to build one. He and Auntie Helen were back at Bingham! What a comfort it was to see them every day. Auntie Helen and I relived the days when I was one of "her girls." Their son, Russ (Van), was visiting them from Canada that year. A classmate of Murray's, he was able to relate to the boarding school experience and we all enjoyed getting to know him. Realizing what a treat it would have been to have Murray, Brian or Carolee with us, I was very happy that Uncle Bill and Auntie Helen could have this wonderful privilege of Russ' visit.

The new dorm gradually took shape in front of our eyes. It was a long, two-storey building behind the main building, with staff apartments on the lower floor. Two long ramps went up to the girls' dorms on the right and the boys' dorms on the left. Downstairs in the centre was a living room where the students could lounge or have special events together. Right behind the building the eucalyptus forest stretched to the fence. We were able to move into it after Christmas. Sadly, that meant the Schmidts had to move on for their next project.

Mr. Wallace was the principal and taught Grades Eight and Nine. He was a no-nonsense teacher who had excellent class control. I was a little nervous around him but he also struck me funny. One day the Grade Nines were all whispering and snickering during an algebra test, so he announced, "All right, five marks off all your papers…except Lynn." Lynn (the Emmels' daughter) hadn't been talking.

Later, as he marked the tests, he said without looking up, "Lynn, by not talking you doubled your mark!" I could see her roll her eyes and laugh, not only at her mark but at the fact that she was the well-behaved one this time. She was funny and mischievous, not afraid of anything, even though some of her antics almost landed her in trouble. I envied her, since I was still always nervous at the thought of doing something wrong.

We older girls were all assigned a Grade One girl as our "little sister." Naturally, Sharilyn was mine. I helped her adjust to the rules, keep her drawer clean, and decide what to wear. The worst part of the job was being responsible to wash and curl her hair. Her hair was almost shoulder length and Mom had given her a tight perm before school started. After washing it, I had to spend almost half an hour trying to get the tangles out of her hair before curling it, while she winced and yelped at my tugging. One Saturday, I became so frustrated I gave up and told her I wasn't going to curl it and just left the tight curls to dry. Unfortunately, the next day a picture was taken of her class for the yearbook. I felt terrible but as it turned out, she didn't look too bad in the picture after all.

That term, I spent a lot of time with Joy Anderson, a kindred spirit whom I had known since pre-school. Joy had graduated from Bingham but was taking Grade Ten by correspondence. Joy and I were alike in so many ways, which is why we enjoyed being together so much. It seemed we spent most of our time talking about the crushes we had on our boyfriends. "Boyfriend" to us meant stealing looks at a guy across the room and giggling about it later. We never as much as held their hands and were ecstatic if we merely caught them looking back at us.

Joy and I loved to play the piano together and sing. We soon formed a trio with our friend, Helen Hay (daughter of the Hays, founders of Bingham). We asked Carol Wallace (Mr. Wallace's daughter) to play the piano for us. We spent many hours singing together, often fooling around and laughing hysterically more than singing.

Carol, Julene, Joy, Helen

Now that Daddy lived in Addis, he could come out to Bingham more often. If the staff knew ahead of time, he was often asked to tell the whole school a story during "story hour," as he had done many times over the years. This had been a tradition for as long as we could remember when "Mr. Hodges" happened to be in Addis. He would prepare for the story just as he would a sermon, taking notes, studying details, practising. Sometimes they were missionary stories he had read, other times a tale from the Reader's Digest. He was a skilful storyteller and the whole school sat in rapt attention as he made

165

the tale come alive. We Hodges kids always burst with pride for a day or two afterwards as people raved about our dad's storytelling.

In the New Year, 1965, Mr. Wallace told us that on February 1st Queen Elizabeth would be making a state visit to Ethiopia. He said he was going to take a whole bunch of students to town to see her. I raced to the dorm after school and hooted, jumping up and down and hugging everyone in sight. Could anything so exciting ever be happening? To top it all off, it would be on my fourteenth birthday!

On our station at Bobeecho, Auntie Fiona always had books and magazines about the royal family, which her family back in Britain sent to her. I went over to her house again and again, begging to look at them. I spent hours memorizing every detail of the royal wedding dresses, the hats, the tiaras and the palaces. Now the real live Queen was coming to Ethiopia!

February 1st finally arrived and we waited on the side of the processional route with thousands of other people, standing on tiptoes and straining to see over the crowds. Finally, an ornate black carriage drove by, pulled by six white horses. Inside, King Haile Selassie sat straight and regal with his high, plumed hat, and the Queen sat beside him, waving. In just a few a seconds they were gone. She wore a pink and yellow dress with a yellow coat. Her hat was made of pink and yellow flowers. I had never heard of wearing pink and yellow together before and decided on the spot that it was the prettiest colour combination I had ever seen.

If I thought that was exciting, it was nothing compared to what happened the next day. All members of the Commonwealth were invited to attend a garden party with the Queen and Prince Philip. I dressed in my prettiest dress and Mr.

Wallace drove those of us from Bingham who had been invited to the British Embassy. We stood on a well-mowed, grassy field behind a low ribbon barrier, filled with excitement for our glimpse of royalty. I found Mom and went to stand beside her. People gradually filed in, the ladies dressed in their fancy clothes with hats and gloves, waiting with anticipation.

Finally, a large old Rolls Royce drove up and as the car door opened, I held my breath. When the Queen stepped out, the whole crowd drew in a gasp. She was only thirty-nine years old and looked so young. She had the most flawless white skin and wore a turquoise coat and hat. She immediately turned her smile on the gathered crowd and began to walk slowly along, talking to people and listening intently as they replied to her. I was standing at the front and could barely contain my excitement as I realized she would have to walk right by me. I waited with my camera poised.

Mom (far left) talks to the Queen

She came within inches of me and stopped. Then she started to talk to my mom right beside me! I raised my camera to take a picture but that felt very rude, so I lowered it again. An insistent thought changed my mind, *She doesn't know you and you need a picture to keep for the rest of your life!* So, with hands shaking, I took a picture. Then I noticed that everyone else was taking pictures too, and the Queen didn't seem to mind at all.

From that day on, I became passionate about everything royal. I began a scrapbook, pasting in pictures of her visit to Ethiopia. A lot of missionaries received Time Magazine and in it was a little section on one page called "People." There, I could almost always count on something being written about someone royal, often with a picture attached and I would ask if I could cut out the picture for my scrapbook. People soon learned about my collection and Bingham friends and missionaries sent me pictures from all over the country. I was so touched. (That little section on one page in the Time magazine turned out to be so popular, years later it became a whole magazine called "People.")

In my first semester of Grade Eight, Bingham was unable to find a piano teacher for the older girls. After a search, Mr. Wallace found Mme. de Sula, who agreed to teach us. She was Russian, married to a French diplomat and a former concert pianist. Five of us would go to her house every week. (Besides taking lessons we would also finish off all the candies from a bowl on her coffee table).

When she assigned one of us a piece of music – Chopin, Rachmaninoff or Beethoven – she always played it for us first. We sat open-mouthed and spellbound, watching her nimble fingers fly all over the keyboard. Although she hadn't played a concert for many years, she hadn't lost any of her skill. She played with intense feeling and expression, as though she loved every note.

She gave me Chopin Waltz #11 in G Flat to learn. It was the most difficult piece I had ever been given but I practised it for hours and hours. I was determined to learn it because I had been completely inspired by her playing, and because the piece was so beautiful. Mom loved it, too, and couldn't hear me play it enough, mistakes and all. I was very self-conscious, though, because she kept asking me to play it for others.

"But, Mom," I groaned, "I don't know it well enough."

"Oh, Julene, we don't care. Come on, play it for us."

In the second semester, Miss Bevington was our piano teacher. She was a new missionary, quiet and reserved. I really enjoyed my lessons and many days found me visiting her in her apartment at Bingham. She assigned me "Claire de Lune" for the June recital. This was a family favourite. Brian and Carolee both played it and all the Dewar family, including Mom, had always loved it.

Now that I was the oldest daughter "at home," Mom took me to the market to choose some material for a new dress for the recital on the last day of school. After searching through many shops filled with fabric, I finally chose a gorgeous blue sparkling organza. It didn't help calm my nerves a bit when I played "Claire de Lune" at the recital but I loved the dress so much that I declared I wanted Mom to make my wedding dress out of sparkling organza when I got married, which she did.

A day or so after graduation, a huge bus came to Headquarters. A large number of families were due to go home on furlough and the mission had rented a bus to take them to the airport and chartered a plane to fly those who were going to North America. As the men loaded suitcases onto the bus, little

169

kids raced around and the adults had final visits with one another. I stood off to one side, dreading this goodbye. So many friends were leaving that day. I had been in the same classes and dorms with them since starting Bingham and I knew I might never see them again.

After the bus pulled out of the Headquarters compound that afternoon, I ran to my room and cried myself to sleep. When I woke up, my dear friend, Joy, found me, put her arm around me and comforted me. I was so happy she hadn't gone. We spent the rest of the afternoon talking together, playing the piano and dreaming of what our lives would hold in the future. Joy had a way of saying things that made me laugh until my stomach ached and soon I was cheered up.

That summer our family took a holiday trip to Bishoftu, about an hour's drive from Addis. Bishoftu was a beautiful vacation spot that the mission provided where people could relax and take their holidays. The property sloped steeply down to the edge of a small crater lake. Dotted along the steep hillside were cottages, almost hidden among the forest of fruit trees, tall poinsettia bushes, fragrant oleanders and cascading bougainvillea vines.

To my delight, a very special friend from Bingham, Nancy Ackley, was there. Her parents were actually missionaries to Sudan but were having difficulty obtaining visas to go there, so the mission had asked them to work meanwhile at Bishoftu. Nancy was a description of the word "fun" and I spent the whole time with her. In her parents' cottage, we found a big stash of "Ideals" magazines, old-fashioned books with the most beautiful and nostalgic pictures. She and I came upon a box of tangerines one day and ate the entire box as we read and visited together.

We also swam in the crater lake, which was twenty feet deep at the dock and two hundred feet deep in the middle. Someone had purchased a huge inner tube and we spent sunburned hours with other kids playing on it, pushing each other off and trying to stay on. Other times we read books, played the piano, or played games in the main living room.

Each family at Bishoftu stayed in a separate cottage. For meals we all ate together in a common dining room. In the evenings after supper, almost everyone gathered outside to play volleyball as the sun was setting. Our family was able to spend four glorious weeks there, enjoying the other missionary families who came and went. Being able to stay at Bishoftu was a distinct highlight of every missionaries' kid's life in Ethiopia.

After our vacation, we went with Mom and Daddy back to Bobeecho, since they had finished their temporary work in Addis. I had really enjoyed our time in Addis but oh, how good it felt to be home in Bobeecho again!

There was a new family on the station now, the Stinsons.

They had a little boy, Dave, a girl, Sherry and a baby, Doug. Sharilyn and Sherry, almost the same age, played all day together.

Mom told me that Auntie Muriel Stinson was the one of the most thoughtful people she knew. Since we had no phones, sometimes she would send a note to Mom, and I used to look at it, thinking that she had the loveliest handwriting. I often wondered if there was some way I could imitate the way she wrote.

Uncle Lloyd Stinson worked hard at learning the local dialect, Hadiya. Eventually, he was even able to preach in the language. Most missionaries would have been happy just to master Amharic.

In June, before the school year ended, Joy had invited me to come to her station, Soddu, for a couple of days at the end of the holidays. I had happily agreed but as August drew to a close, I walked around with a lump in my throat for days. How could I ever have agreed to leave Mom and Daddy early, even if it was to visit my dear friend? I hadn't stopped to think how every single day with them seemed too precious to give up. I felt like I had betrayed them. To make matters worse, Mom was experiencing the same sadness I was. Once I arrived at Soddu, though, it was so much fun to see Joy again. I loved her parents too and we had a very enjoyable trip back to Addis together.

Chapter Twenty-One

—∞—

Last Year at Bingham

Grade Nine, my last year at Bingham! I was assigned to a wee dorm with Chris Waldock. There was just enough space in the room for one bunk bed, a dresser and a wardrobe. It had a small window that looked out over the ramp to the girls' dorm. Chris had been on furlough the year before. Now, she and I were the only girls in Grade Nine, along with six boys. Our little room was in the brand new building that Uncle Bill Schmidt built, which is still called the "new dorm."

Our dorm supervisor was Mrs. Meed, a young missionary with small children. She was soft-spoken and gentle-mannered and always kind to Chris and me, treating us like adults. She was in charge of several dorms of girls in the new dorm where Chris and I were the oldest.

I knew immediately after settling in that this year was going to be a blast. Chris had so much energy, a ridiculous sense of humour and was so much fun. Plus, she was caring, kind and easy to get along with.

Mr. Wallace taught Grades Eight and Nine again. But this year we had a treat. His wife came in to teach us a couple of subjects - Latin and English. I looked forward to every time she came in. I copied the Latin conjugation of verbs she wrote on the board and shook my head, wondering why I was enjoying Latin, a dead language, so much? But then, who had as nice a teacher as Mrs. Wallace? She also taught us Shakespeare's "Twelfth Night."

I had a lot of trouble with some of my subjects that year, particularly Math and Science. The one subject I always enjoyed was Bible. We studied the book of Isaiah in Grade Nine. When it came time for our exam, I went down to a secluded place in the forest and memorized all the notes Mr. Wallace had given us, including the divisions of the book and its major details.

When I went to write the test, the first question read, "Give an outline of the book of Isaiah." I smiled at how fortunate I was to have learned that and began to write. I soon filled a whole page of the things I had memorized.

The next day, just before Mr. Wallace handed our tests back, he went over the first question with the class. He picked up my paper and read my whole answer, ending by saying, "Now *that* was what I was looking for." I smiled at him in delight. I had done well in one of my subjects. I blushed with joy as he handed my paper back to me.

The Hays were back again at Bingham as the station heads, after having worked in northern Ethiopia for a few years. Mrs. Hay asked me to teach Sunday School to the Grade Two class, which had about twenty students, including Sharilyn. Before long, I guessed that most of the kids didn't know what it meant to be saved. So I enthusiastically explained to them about salvation, telling them how important this decision was. I then invited any who wanted be saved to remain after the class, signalling to Sharilyn that I expected her to be among them. Several stayed afterwards to pray with me. Sharilyn looked up to me as her heroine, and would have done anything I said, so she asked Jesus into her heart along with the others; but she never forgot the day she made that decision.

The end of March 1966, the Mission's Council voted Daddy in as Director of East Africa SIM so he and Mom

moved to Addis. Although I never got over my homesickness for Bobeecho, I was glad to be living once again at Headquarters. It was a fun place, always bustling with activity. All the staff ate together in a common dining room, and Ethiopian staff and visitors joined us for tea times. Missionaries were always coming and going to and from their stations all over the country. Now Sharilyn and I could be there every weekend. To make matters even more exciting, Chris' parents were asked to come on staff at Headquarters too, which meant I could spend the whole summer with her.

While Daddy was up in Addis for the March council meetings, he talked to Mr. Wallace about what I should do after graduating from Bingham. Mr. Wallace told him that he had enrolled his daughter and son, Carol and Pete, in the French School just a couple of blocks away from Headquarters. He felt that because they were from Canada, a bilingual country, it would be beneficial for them to spend a year learning French. Daddy agreed it was a great idea and immediately went and enrolled me.

175

I was horrified when he told me and burst into tears. I had struggled all year with French and had my heart set on going to Good Shepherd School, where Joy was taking Grade Eleven and where Chris would be going after graduating from Bingham. But he stood his ground and assured me it would be a very good experience for me, adding that Helen Hay would be attending there as well.

Mom and Daddy moved to Addis in April and settled into an apartment on the main floor. It was two rooms at the end of a long, outdoor walkway along the front of the main building. Their rooms had high ceilings and a wall of windows and French doors looking down over a lawn and garden at the back of the Headquarters compound. Mom placed a long planter in front of the lace-curtained French doors and arranged the family's books in the bookcases on either side of a fireplace on the opposite wall. We came across a bullet hole in one shelf that had happened during the coup of 1960. Aunt Julene and Uncle Buzz sent us a gift of money to be able to buy furniture in Addis. What a treat it was to have furniture that for the first time was not homemade! Mom and Daddy placed the couch and chairs in front of the bookcases with decorative tables here and there. Daddy could walk right out from the apartment into his office across the walkway.

The front room faced the courtyard where beautiful bougainvillea-covered stone pillars lined the walkway. The back room of the apartment was Mom and Daddy's bedroom, a large room, containing a sink, fridge and a small table at the foot of their bed, where we ate our breakfasts. Mom placed her desk and sewing machine in front of the windows. She spent many hours working and sewing in that room.

There was a large room at the end of another long hall off the outdoor walkway, which became Sharilyn's and my bedroom. Its tall window looked down over a narrow stone pathway that led to the laundry room in the basement below us. By the pathway was a high stone wall over which we could see a maze of rusted tin roofs and hear the blare of radios and traffic. We each had a bed on either side of the room and Mom sewed lovely curtains and bedspreads for us. Daddy cut a doorway through the wall to join our room to their apartment. Sharilyn and I loved going to be with them every weekend and settled happily into our room.

It didn't seem long before June arrived and time for exams. In our classroom, Mr. Wallace put on a large reel-to-reel tape of Haydn's Trumpet Concerto as we wrote, which I found calming. I was sure no other schoolteacher gave his students such a treat.

When recital and graduation day finally arrived, Mom took Chris and me, two excited young ladies, to her own hairdresser. Maria carefully styled and sprayed our hair to perfection.

Later, in our wee dorm, Chris and I gently eased our recital dresses over our coiffed hair. The day in my life had finally arrived when I could wear a corsage!

A couple of ladies had picked gladiolus flowers from the profuse abundance of Headquarters' flower gardens and lovingly fashioned two corsages, each tied with a bow. They brought them to Bingham and pinned them on our dresses, dark pink for Chris and yellow for me. I stood back to look at Chris and thought I had never seen her look more stunning than she did now in her baby-blue dress with its white lace top. Mom and Daddy had given me a crystal necklace for graduation and Mom hooked it around my neck and straightened the over-the-shoulder collar on my green dress one last time. We were ready for our big day.

Being in the graduating class, we had to wait for the whole school to finish playing their recital pieces. We each gave our graduation speeches, on which we had laboured long and hard. Mark Middleton's was so funny he had people practically falling off their chairs in laughter. Finally, it was time for me to play my recital piece – Chopin's Military Polonaise in A. I was grateful that Grace Scheel, my beloved piano teacher, had worked so hard with me so that my nervousness and trembling hands didn't keep me from playing it almost perfectly. (And yes, my foot shook.) It was a loud, flamboyant song and a most appropriate, thunderous end to my piano career at Bingham.

When the ceremony and picture taking was all over, we grads stood around talking of our futures. None of the boys in the class was going to stay in Ethiopia except Peter Wallace, and we were all reluctant to say goodbye to one another. We had been together for most of our nine grades – years of happy, sad, hilarious and painful memories – and shared so much in common of the unusual life of a missionaries' kid. So we all stood around and talked with a closeness we had never dared show before and finally hugged one another and said goodbye.

Peter Wallace, Dan Maxson, Mr. Wallace, Stan Kayser, Jerry Healy
Mark Middleton, Julene, Chris Waldock, Brian Isaacs

That summer, at Headquarters, Chris and I did everything together. We had sleepovers in an attic we discovered; we went uptown to look through shops. Because it was rainy season, we also stayed inside for days and played Rook until we were ready

179

to climb the walls. On sunny days, we ran around Headquarters begging everyone we saw to take us to Bishoftu. Every now and then someone who had business at Bishoftu would agree to take us. We spent the day swimming, boating and sun-tanning with families who were there vacationing, until it was time to come home.

Back home in Canada, Murray and Brian were in final preparations to be married (six weeks apart). No matter how much we longed to go to their weddings, missionaries just did not travel home for such things in those days. When Murray and Carol's wedding day arrived, July 23rd, 1966, Mom figured out exactly when it would start in Ethiopian time. I lay in bed all night, thinking of Carol walking down the aisle, of Murray so handsome in his suit, of Carolee in her pink satin bridesmaid dress and of all our loved ones who would be there.

Mom had written home to family and friends, begging them to send details of the wedding for us, saying, "Let none of you say, 'You've probably already heard about Murray and Carol's wedding so I won't bother'. Please tell us everything you can think of." Many responded with long and newsy letters and we treasured every word.

The weeks passed and we waited and waited for the wedding pictures. We were still waiting for them when Brian and Rose were married on September 3rd. I spent another long night dreaming of every aspect of their wedding. It turned out that Brian's pictures arrived before Murray's. That was the happiest day we could imagine. For hours, we sat together on the couch, looking at the pictures over and over, memorizing every detail, trying to identify every person, exclaiming at how beautiful Rose was and how lovely Carolee looked, how handsome Brian was, and best of all, the wonderful picture of our new, growing family – Murray and Carol, Brian and Rose and Carolee.

Finally, Murray and Carol's pictures arrived. More days of absolute delight were spent looking at them and enjoying them in exactly the same way we had treasured Brian and Rose's.

In late August my Grade Ten English and Science courses arrived from the Alberta Correspondence School. Mom and Daddy felt that I should take those subjects because I would be studying only French and Math at the French school. Mom immediately picked up my English textbook and was soon curled up on the couch, reading and exclaiming over the stories and poems. She was to be my English teacher that year and coached me with great enthusiasm and interest as we read, laughed over and endlessly discussed the stories together. Being such a good writer herself, she was a marvellous help to me as I wrote essays and assignments.

The time arrived for me to begin Grade Ten. I was the only child in our family to be able to stay in Ethiopia so long.

.

Chapter Twenty-Two

French School – Teenager in Addis

A rooster crowed as the Addis sky started to lighten. Climbing out of bed, I pulled back the curtain, opened the tall window, and leaned out, wanting to feel the wind blowing on my face. I could smell smoke from the many fires cooking food in homes all over the city. One of my favourite laundry ladies looked up and waved at me from the stone path below as she unlocked the laundry room door. Mom and I so appreciated the work they did for us and I could tell all the laundry ladies adored Mom and loved hearing her speak Amharic to them on our many visits to pick up our clothes.

Today would be my first day at the French School. I dressed and went into Mom and Daddy's bedroom to give them hugs. Mom had started making breakfast so I sat at the little table at the foot of their bed, enjoying the aroma of toast and coffee.

Daddy sat down at the other side of the table. "I'm going to get Donna to send out invitations to all staff in Addis for another day of prayer," he said. Being Director for so many missionaries was a big job for him, and he carried their struggles on his heart. All his life he had been a strong believer in prayer, so he began to call for regular days of prayer for all those who worked in different parts of Addis. He also began an early-morning prayer meeting each Friday to pray for specific problems, such as the trouble that some missionaries were having obtaining visas to work in Ethiopia.

"I don't think I'll go out to the little shack at the Girls Christian Academy compound to pray on Saturdays any more," he continued. "It's too far from HQ (Headquarters). I think I'll just use Room 16." Mom nodded as she buttered the toast. Room 16 was a tiny room at the top of a long flight of stairs beside Headquarters' dining room. With its single bed, table and basin and small wardrobe, it reminded me of Elisha's "prophet's chamber." Daddy made a habit of praying and fasting there every Saturday.

He turned to me and grabbed my hand, "Ju, are you excited for the French School?"

"I think so," I replied, "but I don't have any idea what to expect. Carol, Pete and Helen should be here in about half an hour."

When they arrived from Bingham, Pete took off on his own. We three girls sauntered down the lower hill and greeted the watchman as he opened the back gate for us then walked on down the road as it angled toward the river, chatting about what this year might be like. We ran across the bridge, pausing to look across busy Churchill Road at the French School on the other side.

Churchill Road was a main thoroughfare in Addis, which led up a steep hill to "uptown" and we had to look both ways and be alert as we crossed it. We knew where our classroom was – a brick building at the bottom of the hill, right beside the lower gate. When we tried to enter, a guard stopped us and told us we would have to walk all the way to the top of the hill and use the gate up there. Annoyed, we grumbled and started up the hill.

We found the gate at the top and walked down a long

183

pathway past the many buildings of the French School – past classrooms where people really could speak French. On our way, we passed a stone wall, on which a group of older boys sat talking and laughing. We were all wearing below-the-knee skirts, which looked like they had come straight out of missionary barrels. Being stylish was not something that had ever crossed our minds before. The boys started snickering as we walked by. Suddenly, one of them began chanting, "*A la mode*" (which means "up-to-date fashion" in French) over and over and all the others joined in. We hurried down the hill. What was wrong with that guard at the lower gate anyway? Why couldn't we have gone in there and saved ourselves this persecution? We had to endure this kind of teasing the whole year.

In our classroom, M. Boudon, a short, stout, red-faced man with thinning, unruly blond hair, greeted us. He showed us to our seats at the very back of the big classroom, with its high ceilings and tall windows standing open on one wall. Carol and Pete sat in a double desk across the aisle from Helen and me, who were sharing another desk. The whole classroom had double desks. Other students gradually filed in and M. Boudon began telling us what to do. We didn't understand a word he said.

Our class was called "*Troisieme D'Acceuil*," which meant the "Third Welcome" class for older students who wanted to learn French. Right from the first moment, he began to correct our pronunciation of "*Monsieur*," since we all said, "Meh-shur" instead of "Meh-syeuh."

After that, we realized that he was asking us our nationalities. All over the class, we heard students say, "Yugoslavia, Israel, England, Syria, Denmark, Sweden, U.S., Italy, Ethiopia" and, of course, "Canada." Carol, Pete and I were from Canada, and Helen was from the States but M. Boudon always called the four of us his *"Canadiens."* It turned out our class was made up of fourteen different nationalities.

It took a few weeks before we began to understand our teacher or his wife, who came in twice a week to teach us geometry. Mme. Boudon looked very European and had long fingernails, which continually scratched the blackboard as she wrote on it. At first, we cringed and put our hands over our ears every time she wrote on the board but after hearing the sound for months, we actually became used to it. Her hair was dyed black, she wore bright red lipstick, and she was the same height as her husband. She was quiet and reserved.

M. Boudon, on the other hand, had an emotional personality and was easily exasperated. He would fly into a rage when someone hadn't written neatly or done work to his satisfaction, pick up his or her notebook, tear it in half and fling it across the room. Afterward, he would calm right down and continue on up the aisle, helping other students. We never felt threatened by him. Instead, we thought he was hilarious.

Gradually, we became acquainted with our fellow students, many of them with very different, often delightful, personalities. Most of them spoke English. In front of Carol and Pete sat Nina and Mats, a brother and sister from Denmark who already spoke fluent Danish, Swedish and English – and now were learning French. In front of Helen and me was a petite American girl, Donna, with a cute upturned nose and dimpled smile. She wore miniskirts, as did most of the other girls in the class, unlike the three of us in our long, old-fashioned skirts.

M. Boudon constantly assigned us long recitations in French and we would slave away at memorizing the words, barely knowing what they meant. He spent a lot of time correcting our pronunciation, which thrilled my mom when I told her, because she always thought a language should be learned with the most perfect pronunciation possible. From time to time, I would try to teach Mom some French words then would roll my eyes at her. "Mom, you always say all these French words with an Amharic accent," I groaned.

The French School classes lasted until 1:00 p.m. each day. Back at HQ, I then had to work on English and Science correspondence courses. English was very enjoyable with Mom; Science I didn't understand at all and I just despised it. I was not a disciplined student either, so Daddy made it his responsibility to keep me at my lessons. He would sometimes shake his head and say, "I need to hire two new missionaries – one to keep you working and one to keep the maintenance man at his job."

Although he had to get after me a lot, he was also very kind about it. One day I wrote in my diary, "Here if I wasn't an old grouch, sassing Daddy about doing Science and just being plain HORRID. A little while later he comes to see what I'm doing, and finding me working on Science, makes me a cup of cocoa and crackers with honey."

Eventually, Daddy asked the Science teacher at Bingham, Mr. Giles, if he would help me. Each week I would catch a ride with someone out to Bingham, and Mr. Giles would go over my exercises with me. His apartment was on the lower floor of the new dorm, where he lived with his wife and four sons. One day as he was helping me, one of his sons was playing in another room with a friend. One of them let out the loudest burp. Mr. Giles was explaining something to me, and without even pausing in his sentence, he said, "Pardon the pig" and went on. I wanted so badly to burst out laughing but I knew it would be terribly rude. So I bit my lip, held my breath, struggled not to laugh and tried my hardest to keep listening.

When I finally finished my lesson with him, I thanked him. Tearing out of his house, I raced over to Grace Scheel's apartment. I burst in her door, collapsed on the couch and laughed until I could laugh no more. She had absolutely no idea why but stared at me with a puzzled look until I finally calmed down enough to tell her.

Grace had become a great friend after having been my piano teacher in Grade Nine. She was a young missionary, the same age as Murray, and was so much fun. Her brother, Dick, was a mission doctor and her nephew, Dan, had been in my grade at Bingham. I loved spending time with her.

In October, Mr. Hay, who with his wife had started Bingham Academy twenty years before, had a stroke and was rushed to the hospital. The whole mission held its breath, as did Bingham Academy and all the Ethiopians who had worked with him and loved him so much.

I kneeled by my bed that evening and prayed, "God, I wish I knew how to have faith, so I could pray for him." (One of my memory verses at Bingham had been "All things whatsoever ye shall ask in prayer, *believing*, ye shall receive..")

A day or so later, Mr. Hay passed away peacefully and Mom and Auntie Evelyn Brant prepared his body for burial. The next day the HQ chapel was filled to capacity, with people standing in the back and outside. My heart just ached for Helen, as I saw her being so brave, sitting with her mom in the front row. We went out to a cemetery afterwards for his burial and watched the pallbearers lower him into the grave. When they began to throw dirt on his coffin, Helen started to cry, and I blinked back the tears.

Dear, dear, Helen, one of the sweetest friends I'd ever known, only seventeen, would be without a daddy for the rest of her life.

A couple of days later, back at school, M. Boudon came over to Helen's and my desk, and put his hand gently on her shoulder.

"Your fah-zer die?" he asked softly, the only English words I ever heard him speak. Helen nodded, tears brimming in her eyes as I reached for her hand under our desk. I just couldn't imagine how terrible it would be to lose my daddy.

Chapter Twenty-Three

—∞—

HQ Days

A lively hymn sing was in full swing at HQ. The song director asked for one favourite after another and it seemed the congregation wanted to sing all night. A couple of vans from Bingham had brought the Grades Seven to Nine students, and they sat here and there in the chapel along with visitors from different organizations in Addis who joined us.

Mr. Harbottle, a British man from the Red Sea Mission Team, was playing the piano. No matter what the mood of the song, he changed from fast to slow, playing with such ease in many different styles. I was sitting beside Mom, who raved about his playing, especially when he accompanied the choir, in which she sang. She whispered to me between songs, "He can read any music perfectly at first sight. I love his lovely rippling runs in thirds and his thunderous wanderings in the bass. And he's so likable." I had to agree with her. Everything he played was a treat to hear.

Mom asked Mr. Harbottle if he would be my piano teacher that year. He was a kind and patient teacher. The pieces he gave me were difficult and took a lot of practice. I would spend an hour or more each afternoon in the HQ chapel, underneath the guest rooms, practising on the old yellow piano with its nice, mellow tone. Sometimes a guest, curious to know who was playing, would come in to look, which always embarrassed me, and the door was left open when he or she left. I would then

189

have to get up from the piano, walk all the way across the front of the auditorium and close the door. Finally, I just borrowed a knife from the kitchen, and jammed it into the doorframe so nobody could come in.

In January, Mr. Harbottle assigned me Beethoven's Pathetique Sonata, a 32-page piece that I worked on so much that I eventually learned it by heart. Helen, Carol and Pete also took lessons from him but I was enormously relieved he did not make us have a recital that year.

I was asked to play the piano quite often for church at HQ now, too. Sometimes I was scolded for playing much too fast but people were forgiving and sang heartily. Mom always sat in her seat beaming with pride as she watched me. I had to find a new "offertory" each week – special music to be played during offerings. Now all the things Grace Scheel had taught me in Grade Nine about playing hymns so they would sound like solos were put to good use. My sister-in-law, Carol, sent me books of hymn transcriptions from Canada. What a delightful gift. They were beautiful arrangements, full of fancy, unusual chords.

Mom was not the Hostess at HQ but at times she was asked to assist if the Hostess was away. She would go shopping for groceries with the head cook. Chris and I often asked to go with her to the market. One day, to my delight, I discovered some eyebrow pencil in a little shop, bought it, and ran over to show Chris. "Are you going to wear makeup?" she gasped, eyes wide. We both knew a lot of missionaries considered wearing make-up a sin.

"Well, we should be able to wear just a little, right?"

Eyebrow pencil wasn't enough for me, though. I decided to look in the market for mascara but never found any. One day I had the brightest idea. "I'm going to wear black shoe polish on my eyelashes," I told Chris, who shook her head in disbelief. From then on, I carefully coated my eyelashes each day with shoe polish.

Soon my eyes became red and sore. Puzzled, I innocently told Mom about it and she took me to Dr. Adair. She checked my eyes but could find no obvious problem. After a few questions, she asked me if I wore makeup. "Not much," I said.

"Well, try going without it for a while and see if that helps."

After I left her office, it dawned on me that maybe the shoe polish was the cause. I ran to tell Chris about my doctor's appointment. She threw back her head and laughed. "Not much, huh?"

On my many trips to Bingham for Science tutoring, I loved to spend time with Jacque Konnerup, who was now in the Grade Nine graduating class. When we were together, we were about as crazy as two teenagers could possibly be and I always looked forward to being with her. She told me that she was going to Good Shepherd after she finished Bingham, because she was an American.

Good Shepherd School was formed by several missions such as the Baptist Mission, the American Mission, the Mennonite Mission, etc. that wanted an American curriculum for their children. I really wanted to go to Good Shepherd, too. I was happy that I was learning French, and thrilled that I could understand just about everything M. and Mme. Boudon said now; but I didn't want to go to the French School another year and I *sure* didn't want to take correspondence courses again.

I felt so spoiled being able to live with Mom and Daddy and enjoyed them more than ever before. I know they loved having a teenager living in Ethiopia with them, too. Mom and I

191

became closer and closer friends, spending a lot of time in each other's company and enjoying so many similar things.

Mom kept busy creating Bible courses and doing translation work. She even began teaching Amharic language classes for new missionaries who worked in Addis, which she thoroughly enjoyed. She also loved it when she could take trips down country to hold women's meetings, riding "out into the bush." She thrived on being able to go trekking again, visiting and teaching the women.

When she was asked to help with the job of HQ Hostess, it kept her very busy – planning meals, shopping and working with the Ethiopian staff, meeting guests and assigning them to their rooms. One thing I knew she liked about living at HQ was being able to dress up for the first time in her missionary career.

Daddy also had to do a lot of travel. He attended conferences. He visited mission stations, where he often had to help solve problems. When he came back to Addis, his faithful secretary, Donna Cottrell, would present him with a pile of letters, urging him to set aside some time to dictate answers. Although he said he always felt his first priority was helping missionaries, he tried to make time each morning for writing letters.

When Daddy was first chosen to be Director, he and Mom prayed and agreed together that, with God's help, they would not in any way speak evil of anyone. As a result, I tended to think that all missionaries were just about perfect – I never heard otherwise in our home.

Being at HQ, and eating meals in the main dining room, I got to know everyone in the mission quite well, since all of them had to come up from their stations at some time. I looked forward to each day, wondering who would be coming to

Addis. I loved to visit with them over tea and meals, as they told about their work on their stations. We sometimes even had guests from overseas.

Christmas, 1966, the HQ staff busied themselves with preparations for the arrival of the General Director of the mission, Dr. Davis and his wife, from New York. Mr. Borlase spent hours painting the large living room and dining room, and the long, tall arch in between. New pictures appeared on the wall, and old couches and chairs were replaced. When the Davises arrived, they were overwhelmed at all the work that had been done for them, for they were just simple missionaries at heart. They spent the next couple of months visiting many stations in Ethiopia, Somalia and Sudan.

Mr. Borlase, the mission's Deputy Director, was a huge encouragement to Daddy. He was a tall, slim man, balding, with a thick moustache. There was always a mischievous twinkle in his eye. One day after dinner, we were walking out of the dining room together when his wife tripped on a rug and fell on her knees. Horrified that Mr. Borlase did not reach down to help her get up, I cried out, "Mr. Borlase, is chivalry dead?"

From then on, he would go ahead of me to open doors, make a sweeping bow and say, "See, Julene, chivalry is not dead." To top it off, he gave me a whole box of Juicy Fruit gum for Christmas. Maybe he thought that would keep me from running into his office to ask for it!

The Borlases never had children but they adopted the mission's kids as their own. The Binghamites adored Mr. Borlase because whenever he came out to Bingham, he told amusing stories and said such funny things that made us howl with laughter. He was always full of enthusiastic energy. If he were at Bishoftu, he would take groups of us for a day of climbing to the top of Bishoftu Mountain.

Mrs. Borlase, white-haired but young-faced, with a ready smile, was sweetly quiet in contrast to her husband's boisterous friendliness. So Chris and I were thrilled to be able to see them every day at HQ.

Another delightful person who worked at HQ was Ato Lahko. He was an Ethiopian who helped the mission more than could be described, especially in their negotiations with the government offices in Addis. He spoke excellent English, and was just as funny as Mr. Borlase. You can imagine how well the two of them got along.

My mom loved any chance to go visit and laugh with Ato Lahko. He enjoyed and respected her, too. He told me one day that years before he had been very discouraged, almost ready to give up, when he received a letter in the mail from her. She hadn't known he was having problems but merely thought to write him a friendly letter. It was written in Amharic but he couldn't for the life of him figure it out. Finally, it dawned on him that these were English words pronounced the way Ethiopians would say them and written in Amharic script. By the end of the letter he was laughing so hard, it completely cheered him up and his depression lifted.

I often ran upstairs to spend time with Chris in her parents' apartment. They lived on the second floor above Sharilyn's and my room. I thought her dad was very handsome – and a big tease. Her mom was devoted to him and laughed at all his jokes. I told Chris, "I always like watching them together because they are so in love."

On a side table in their living room sat a graduation picture of their oldest daughter, Janet. She smiled serenely and her hair was done perfectly. She was Carolee's age and they had been classmates together at Bingham. Now, like Carolee in Canada, she was living in the States, away from her family. Her picture reminded me of our beautiful grad picture of Carolee proudly displayed on the mantel in our living room.

In June, Carol, Pete, Helen and I finished our year at the French School. We were quite pleased with ourselves that we could now speak French. On the last day of school, an assembly was held for the whole school. Teachers and students rose and gave speeches but to our dismay we hardly understood anything said. Everyone spoke so fast, not slowly and simply like M. and Mme. Boudon. It occurred to us that, far from being as fluent as we had thought, we still had a lot to learn in French. Nevertheless, for the rest of my life I was very grateful for the day that Daddy had gone and enrolled me in the French School.

Chapter Twenty-Four

Last Days in Ethiopia

The rain splattered against the windows of our apartment for the third drizzly day in a row. I said to Mom, who was working at her desk, "I don't remember thinking how dreary rainy season was when I was young. Whatever did we do when it rained like this all the time?"

"You just put on your boots and raincoats and went and played outside, rain or shine," she said. "You never seemed to notice the weather. I guess little kids don't pay any attention to it."

Sharilyn went over to the planter and picked up Herbert, our small chameleon, who crawled slowly around our plants. Placing him on her hand, she pulled back the curtain and held him up to where a fly was buzzing against the window. In a flash, Herbert's long tongue shot out and captured the fly; then he crunched his tasty treat.

"I took Herbert to the big kitchen the other day," Sharilyn said, placing him back on a big leaf in the planter. "I took him to show the cooks. When he stuck out his tongue to eat a bug, they all hollered, 'Oo! I-yee!' and ran away from him as though they had never seen anything like it." We all laughed.

Suddenly, Daddy came in the door, looking happy. "We got a letter from Carolee," he said. We all jumped up and rushed to him. Laughing, he held the letter above his head while we stood on tiptoes trying to grab it out of his hand.

"You already read it, didn't you, Daddy?" said Mom.

"Yep, I did. She says Julene should come home and live

with her or she should come out here for a visit." He handed the letter to Mom. I sat by her on the couch so I could read over her shoulder.

I caught Mom looking wistful and asked her what was wrong. She sighed and said, "I know there was no school available for Murray and Brian when they finished Bingham but if only we had known, maybe Carolee could have come back here for high school and taken correspondence or something."

However, she knew it was no good to waste time regretting the past, so she went back to reading the letter. My mind drifted off as I pondered her words. Rainy season or not, I was overwhelmed at how special it was that I could stay in Ethiopia in my high school years and even *live* with Mom and Daddy. I really missed the rest of our family in Canada but I sure did love living in Ethiopia.

Sharilyn at HQ

Sharilyn came home on weekends from Bingham, and of course stayed with us at HQ all summer. She never lacked for ideas of things to do, regardless of the rain. She loved to put on

197

her roller skates and tear across the parking lot and down the steep hill to the back gate at top speed. At the bottom of the hill were a couple of swings, where she played with friends who were visiting from down country. Sometimes, they would play in our bedroom, and mess up the whole room! She never seemed to grasp how important it was to keep it completely spotless.

That rainy season, to my great delight, Joy's family moved to Addis. They would be living in a stone house down below the main building at HQ. Sadly, Joy and I would have only a few weeks together. Since she had now graduated from Good Shepherd School, she would be going home to the U.S. to begin nurse's training. I vowed I would keep writing to her for life. Her friendship was far too precious to lose.

Joy's parents were from North Carolina. They spoke with a soft southern accent and had gracious southern manners. Uncle Charlie had been in the military when he was young and the tattoo on his arm fascinated all us mission kids. I thought his wife, Auntie Lucille, was the prettiest lady – and as sweet as she was pretty. I adored them. They were so loving to me and treated me like a grown-up even when Joy and I were laughing so hard we couldn't stop.

Beside their stone house "down below" was another stone house where the Hagens lived. They had three boys, John, Matthew and Mark before they finally had a girl, Anna. (That was what we called them; their parents called them by German names.) They first came to Ethiopia when I was in Miss Willey's class and they learned to speak English at Bingham.

A few years later, Mr. and Mrs. Hagen were assigned to work in Addis and asked if they could enrol their kids in a German school. The mission agreed. Even though they lived at

HQ, I didn't see them much because, in typical European fashion, they took summer classes at the French School. However, time spent with the Hagens, whether camping or at Bishoftu, was always a blast. Their boys were incredibly smart and artistic and little Anna was the delight of their whole family.

Mr. Hagen did a lot of shopping for the mission. He would drive back from town into HQ in his van, racing over the speed bumps in the wide driveway down the hill to their house. Once Mom and I were standing out on one of the small patches of green grass in front of the bougainvillaea-covered pillars as he sped by. Mom turned to me and laughed. "He is like Jehu. He 'driveth furiously,'" she said, quoting an Old Testament story.

Mom had her own driving escapades. As I walked home from the French School one day, I was stunned to see that a large part of the stone wall at the bottom end of the HQ compound had collapsed to the ground. The watchman at the gate saw me staring at it with my mouth wide open. "Your mother did it," he said.

"My mother!" I exclaimed in disbelief. He assured me she had and began with great relish to tell me all about it. I didn't know enough Amharic to understand his explanation fully, so I ran up to our apartment, burst through the door, and hollered, "Mom, whatever happened to the back wall?"

"Oh, that," said Mom, looking up from where she sat at her desk, which was covered with paper. Her Amharic Bible lay open on top of English commentaries and books. She quickly wrote a couple more Amharic words in a notebook full of underlined sections with red comments scribbled in the margins. Little pieces of paper, with notes in English and Amharic, were lying here and there.

She put down her pen, shrugged her shoulders and shook

her head. She then stood up and pulled back the sheer curtain on the window in front of her desk, where she could look down the back compound to the broken wall. "I was driving down the hill to the back gate and my brakes completely gave out. I even yanked on the emergency brake but the car kept going faster down the hill. I didn't know what to do because the swings were in the way and there were kids swinging on them but somehow the car missed them and the tree beside them. I crashed into the wall. I sat there and watched as that whole section just crumbled right before my eyes. I could hardly believe it."

"How could a stone wall crumble?"

"It must have originally been put together with mud," she replied. We both stood there in amazement then began to laugh at the ridiculousness of the situation. The car wasn't too badly damaged and the wall was soon fixed, this time with cement between the stones.

The new school year at Good Shepherd School began in September 1967. I ran up the wide outdoor stairs, down the hall to Chris' room, where she was backcombing her hair. Excited, I began talking and asking her questions about GSS. We gathered up our binders, went out near the front gate, where we stood and waited for a van from Bingham.

Quite a few Bingham graduates, whose parents lived down country, were boarded at a "hostel" at Bingham now, in an apartment on the lower floor of the new dorm. Mr. and Mrs. Goss, who at one time worked at Laymo, were asked to be in charge of them. Every morning Mr. Goss would load them up in a van, come to HQ and pick up Chris and me. Then we would all drive out to Good Shepherd together.

Judy Reimer, a quiet friend, had been in Canada for two

years and dressed very stylishly. Eunice Ratzliff, lively and full of laughter, was back in Ethiopia after having been gone for a number of years. She had the most beautiful long eyelashes I'd ever seen on a white person. She and Chris immediately "hit it off" and became great friends. I was convinced that every boy in the entire mission was in love with either Chris or Eunice, because they were so pretty and full of fun.

Lynn Emmel was a senior at Good Shepherd, which meant she was in Grade Twelve. I always enjoyed her adventurous, fun-loving spirit. Jacque Konnerup, freshly graduated from Bingham was a sophomore and I looked forward to being able to see her every day now at school. Three boys, Vernon Bell, Fred Ely and Duane Ediger, all sophomores as well, completed the Bingham group.

The picture below was taken on a special event at Bishoftu, where we spent a glorious weekend together.

Back row: Chris Waldock, Eunice Ratzliff, Julene, Jacque
Konnerup, Lynn Emmel, Judy Reimer
Front row: Fred Ely, Duane Ediger, John Hagen, Vernon Bell

Good Shepherd School went from grades one to twelve, with boarding facilities for those whose parents worked down country. A number of Ethiopians attended the high school, the boys being some of the funniest kids in the school. Also, foreign ambassadors and diplomats to Ethiopia sent their kids to GSS. A well-dressed chauffeur would drive them each up in a fancy car, their country's flag blowing in the breeze on the hood.

The school had an assortment of one-storey buildings scattered here and there over many acres of land. We walked from building to building for our classes, passing each other on sidewalks, joking and laughing together. I had never enjoyed school so much.

The boarding students ate meals together in the school dining room while we day students brought our lunches and ate in spots all over the compound. I befriended a quiet Ethiopian girl named Betty, who always shared her injera and wut with me. Mom faithfully made me lunch every day and I offered some to Betty, feeling a bit guilty because I knew that I got the much better end of the deal.

Mr. Kano, our English teacher, decided to put on a play, "The Crucible," by Arthur Miller. It was a story about the witch trials that took place in Massachusetts in the 1600s. Those of us who joined the Drama Club had parts in it and grew close as we practised for hours together. It was a completely dark, depressing story but we made fun of it, putting the old-English lines from our parts into our conversations as we visited during breaks, laughing uproariously.

In April, Daddy was invited to hold special Easter services at an agricultural college in eastern Ethiopia, a few miles outside the ancient, historic city of Harar. I was happy Sharilyn and I were able to go along, because one of the professors at the college had a daughter who was in my class at GSS, Julie Quenemoen. She was so much fun and would be there for Easter break.

We were driven to Alemaya College, which looked like it was out in the middle of absolutely nowhere, and were shown to our guest rooms. Shortly after we were settled in, there was a knock at the door. A young American man was standing there and he introduced himself. The son of one of the professors, he was studying at the College. It was so seldom that white people, especially girls, came to that location, that when he heard of our arrival, he immediately came for a visit. We were chatting when he turned to Mom and Daddy and asked if he could take me on a date. I was stunned! I was seventeen and had never been on a date in my whole life, and now a total stranger was asking me.

Mom and Daddy must have thought he looked trustworthy, because they agreed. That night, he drove up to our door to pick me up. I was waiting for him, dressed in my Sunday best. I got into the car and we drove to Dire Dawa, a city not too far away. We stopped in front of a restaurant then walked right through it to a small outdoor theatre in the fenced-in back yard, and took our chairs among the trees. While the warm wind blew softly and birds sang, we watched that most wonderful movie, "Sound of Music." I had listened to the record so much that I knew every word to every song. I wanted to sit back and thoroughly enjoy myself. Instead, I felt so nervous I couldn't relax. I didn't know what to expect from a non-missionaries' kid. But he was gallant and thoughtful – a perfect gentleman. I have often thought how very nice my first date was, even though I don't remember the young man's name.

I took piano lessons from Mrs. Radtke at GSS that year, a

lady who had stunning turquoise eyes. She was the first person I ever knew who wore contact lenses. I enjoyed my lessons with her a lot as the year progressed. Suddenly, it was April and she realized she hadn't given me a recital piece yet and assigned me Chopin's Waltz No. 5 in A flat. I took one look at it and realized I was really in trouble. It was five pages long and difficult and I had only two months to learn it. Brian had spent many months learning this same piece on our last furlough.

So, for the months of April and May, I doubled and tripled my practice times on the HQ chapel piano. Hour after hour, I went over and over the complicated runs and passages. I felt sorry for the guests in the rooms above the chapel who had to listen to me drilling the same difficult parts five, ten, twenty times. Sometimes I became so exhausted I would go back to our arpartment, flop on our couch, almost in tears, moaning that I didn't know how I could ever learn it before June. Mom always assured me I was doing fabulously. I looked at her suspiciously. I knew she loved Chopin waltzes so much that I thought maybe she was prejudiced.

June finally arrived and the night before the recital, I went to Mrs. Radtke's house for the rehearsal. When my turn at the piano came, I did the most terrible job, forgetting parts and making mistake after mistake. I almost cried. The next day at the recital, I sat through all the younger kids' pieces, completely depressed. If I had ever dreaded a recital before, it was nothing compared to how much I dreaded playing now. I was so sure I would do badly in front of all those people.

At long last, it was my turn to play. Not even able to manage a smile, I walked all the way up the aisle to the piano, shoulders drooping. I sat down and placed my hands on the keys. Suddenly, energy surged through me and I played page after page almost without a mistake, right down to the last difficult phrase in the song. I blinked in utter astonishment at what had just happened.

Rising from the bench in a daze, I made my way back to my seat, thinking over and over, "I did it! I made it! I'm really finished! It's finally over!" When I slipped into my place beside Daddy, he took my hand, leaned over to me and whispered, "They sure did clap for you." Only then did I look around and see smiles and nods from people all around me.

However, I had worn myself out working on that piece. After the recital, I never looked at it again until years later.

GSS held their graduation exercises that year in a small auditorium in Addis. It was the tradition each year to invite a junior – a Grade Eleven student – to play Elgar's "Pomp and Circumstance" for the graduation march. I longed to be that student more than I could describe. Sure enough, one happy day in May, the music director, Mr. Malloy, came and asked me. I could hardly wait to get back to HQ to tell Mom and Daddy. I practised and practised; even though it was a simple song I wanted learn it absolutely perfectly.

When graduation came, I took my place at the old piano at the front of the auditorium and slowly played the theme as the grads marched up the aisle to the stage in their gowns. It felt like my heart just burst with pride. I must say that, although I have had honours in my life, I do not remember ever feeling more honoured than being able to play that graduation march for the class of '68.

On the last day of school, we received our yearbooks and went around all day asking friends to sign and write something in them. I said goodbye to those who were leaving for good but assured everyone that I would be coming back the next year as a senior. I knew that after I graduated from Grade Twelve the following year, it would be time for Mom and Daddy's furlough, so everything was working out perfectly.

In August, Jean Robertson, a friend from Alberta who had worked in Agaro with my parents decades before, came to Ethiopia. Mom and Daddy were so happy to see her. They visited for hours in their apartment, catching up on news and asking her many questions about Murray and Carol, Brian and Rose, who all lived in Edmonton and went to her church, as well as Carolee who was working there that summer. Being able to entertain someone from home was a rare treat.

During the conversation, Jean asked about my schooling. Mom and Daddy told her I would be finishing high school at an American school. Jean, who was now a Professor at the University of Alberta, thought about it for a minute. "You should consider sending Julene back to Canada for Grade Twelve," she said. "If she wants to go to university, she will need a Canadian diploma."

Mom and Daddy talked it over for a while before they approached me. Meanwhile, in the weeks preceding Jean Robertson's coming, I had been going over a whole bunch of family letters, re-reading the details of Murray and Brian's weddings, looking at their pictures and reliving the occasions. I began feeling homesick for my siblings. So when Mom and Daddy asked if I would consider going back to Canada for Grade Twelve, I said yes, without giving it much thought.

A few days later, we began to make plans for me to leave and the whole situation suddenly hit me. I was leaving Ethiopia! I would be saying goodbye to Mom and Daddy and Sharilyn. What *on earth* was I thinking?

Lunchtime came and I should have gone up to the main

206

dining room to eat with everyone but had completely lost my appetite. Immense homesickness washed over me and I walked around the apartment then sat down on the couch and put my head in my hands. A noise at the front door caught my attention.

There was Mom. I could tell by the look on her face that she was thinking exactly the same thing as I was. I got up and ran into her arms and we both sobbed and cried on each other's shoulders. We were such close friends. How could I ever go? I was leaving so much happiness to face the unknown. And once more, Mom and Daddy would have only Sharilyn.

We had to dry our tears. I had to turn my focus on the positive. I would be able to see Murray and Carol, Brian and Rose and Carolee again. Why, Rose was even expecting her first baby.

Somehow we made it through the next two or three weeks. Daddy's secretary, Donna Cottrell, was going home to the States on furlough and Daddy booked me onto her flights as far as England. From there I would fly over the Arctic to Canada. Eunice Ratzliff was also leaving Ethiopia, along with her older sister, Ruth, who was visiting from North America. Their parents decided to have them fly with Auntie Donna and me.

Mom took me to the market where we picked out fabric to make clothes for me and she began to sew. The dresses even looked a bit stylish, with hems slightly above the knee. We made plans for what I would do in Calgary. I would stay with Aunt Julene and Uncle Buzz until October, when Carolee would come down from Edmonton to begin classes in her final year at Berean Bible College. I would then move into the College and live in a dorm room with her. Mom and Daddy contacted Berean and, since they had known the staff ever since their own Bible College years, they received special permission for me to board there with Carolee while I took Grade Twelve.

Finally, my last day arrived and Daddy helped me close my suitcases. He handed me my ticket and went over the details with me one last time. Sharilyn took my hand, looked up at me and led me out to the car. There, a whole crowd was waiting to say goodbye – missionaries and Ethiopian staff alike, all people whom I had grown to love so much. I tried to hug them all but the biggest embrace was for my dear friend Chris. We promised to write to each other.

When we reached the airport, as I had done so many times in my life, I looked at Mom, Daddy and Sharilyn and gave them a long hug, my throat aching from trying not to cry. Then, I waved goodbye and walked out to the tarmac and up the steps of the Ethiopian Airlines jet.

Finding my seat in the plane, I sat quietly by the window. I saw Mom and Daddy, Sharilyn and the Ratzliffs, who had gone up to the observation deck and were leaning against the railing. As the plane started up its engines, they began to wave. I watched them as a thousand memories flooded my mind.

The plane taxied out, positioning itself for take-off, then roared down the runway and into the air. Mom and Daddy and Sharilyn waved one last time. Below me, the green grasses, the bougainvillea, the people, the eucalyptus trees, the mountains, the beloved thatched-roof huts and everything I loved about Ethiopia became smaller and smaller. It was impossible to believe that chapter in my life had really come to a close.

I sat there watching it all fade from view and prayed, *God, please let me come back to Ethiopia.*

Epilogue

I *was* able to return to Ethiopia. Twenty years later, in November 1988, Mom, Carolee and I went back for a whole month. Our cousin, Dave Hodges, who had become a missionary there with his wife, Rosalie, met us at the airport. Dave told us later he had never seen anyone so excited to come back to Ethiopia. We visited Bingham, Headquarters and Bishoftu but also travelled to Hosanna and Agaro, noting the changes but still able to re-live the dear memories we had of each place. Mom and Daddy had loved the Ethiopians they worked with and were beloved by them. So it should have come as no surprise to us that everywhere we went our old friends were overjoyed to see us. They received us into their homes and prepared feasts for us, treating us like royalty. Mom continued to delight them with her still-perfect Amharic.

In November 1996, I went alone to Ethiopia for Bingham Academy's 50th anniversary reunion and travelled in the country for three weeks. Finally, in April 2010, Murray and I (the most nostalgic of all us kids) went for three weeks. Eager to experience everything Ethiopian again, we visited old mission stations, speaking Amharic, which he does far better than I, and relished every minute we spent together.

In the mid-1970s, a young girl named Marcia Jean became a part of the Hodges family. She has never been to Ethiopia but loves it because we do. She holds a special place in our hearts, especially because of her tender care of our Mom in her final years.

Murray, Brian, Carolee and I all married young, have wonderful spouses, children and grandchildren. Carolee lives in Oregon, U.S.A. and the rest of us in Alberta, Canada.

On December 1, 2004, our baby sister, Sharilyn and her husband Doug were killed in a car accident, leaving two teenage sons. Sharilyn was always such a special gift from God to our family, and her time on earth was far too short. She came long after the rest of us kids, and left before any of us. How we look forward to a grand reunion in heaven with her one happy day.

Daddy passed away in 2001, and Mom in 2008. They are joyfully reunited with Sharilyn and their five children who were buried in Ethiopia, with Fikiray, their adopted baby from Agaro, and with many dear friends from Kaffa and Kambatta as well as the mission. And, best of all, with Jesus whom they so loved, the One who called them to such a wonderful life and ministry in our beloved Ethiopia.

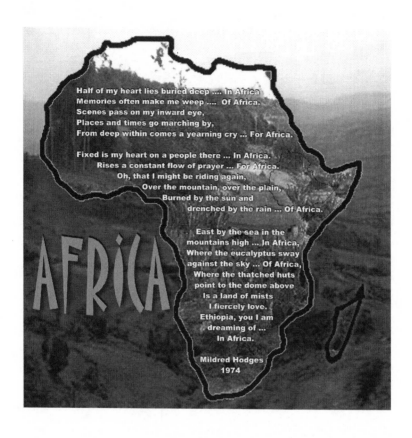

Half of my heart lies buried deep .... In Africa.
Memories often make me weep .... Of Africa.
Scenes pass on my inward eye,
Places and times go marching by,
From deep within comes a yearning cry ... For Africa.

Fixed is my heart on a people there ... In Africa.
Rises a constant flow of prayer ... For Africa.
Oh, that I might be riding again,
Over the mountain, over the plain,
Burned by the sun and
drenched by the rain ... Of Africa.

East by the sea in the
mountains high ... In Africa,
Where the eucalyptus sway
against the sky ... Of Africa,
Where the thatched huts
point to the dome above
Is a land of mists
I fiercely love.
Ethiopia, you I am
dreaming of ...
In Africa.

Mildred Hodges
1974

Artwork by Laura Jacobson Toews

Southern
Ethiopia
1960s

SHOA

To DJIBOUTI ➡

To Harar &
Dire Dawa

Addis Ababa
Bishoftu

KAFFA

Agaro
Jimma

KAMBATTA

Laymo
Hosanna

Duramie

Soddu

ARSI
DESERT

Shashamane
Lake Awassa

Great Rift Valley Lakes

NOTE: Bobeecho station
was about a mile from
Hosanna town and airport